✆✆ COLLAGE FOR THE SOUL ✆✆

ROCKPORT

First published in the United States of America by
ROCKPORT PUBLISHERS, INC.
33 Commercial Street
Gloucester, Massachusetts 01930-5089
Telephone: (978) 282-9590
Fax: (978) 283-2742
www.rockpub.com

Library of Congress Cataloging-in-Publication Data
Harrison, Holly.
   Collage for the soul : expressing hopes and dreams through art /
Holly Harrison and Paula Grasdal.
      p.   cm.
   ISBN 1-56496-962-2 (pbk.)
   1.   Collage. I. Grasdal, Paula. II. Title.
   TT910 .H357 2003
   702'.81'2—dc21   2002011364

ISBN 1-56496-962-2

10 9 8 7 6 5 4 3 2 1

Design: Laura Shaw Design
Cover Image: Bobbie Bush Photography, www.bobbiebush.com
Photographer: Bobbie Bush Photography, www.bobbiebush.com
Proofreader: Pamela Angulo

Printed in Singapore

COLLAGE FOR THE SOUL

Expressing Hopes and Dreams through Art

GLOUCESTER MASSACHUSETTS

ROCKPORT PUBLISHERS

HOLLY HARRISON
and PAULA GRASDAL

CONTENTS

INTRODUCTION

LIKE MOST BOOKS ON THE VAST SUBJECT OF COLLAGE, this one does not claim to be comprehensive. There are several books that contain more about the history of collage and others that offer a wider range of technical information. *Collage for the Soul* differs from those books in that it focuses on using collage to access your inner voice and creativity, offering ideas for getting started, technical guidance, and tips from working artists on refilling your creative well and overcoming creative block. Sidebars provide in-depth looks into various techniques and a bibliography lists useful titles that will inform and inspire artists of all levels.

Collage for the Soul's approach is thematic: Five chapters present twenty-six projects that deal with the topics of expressing personal creativity, exploring and recording relationships, dreaming and wishing, finding inspiration in nature, and creating visual memoirs. Additionally, the instructions tell you how to create a personalized project, sharing necessary techniques while suggesting ideas for substituting your own themes and materials. Rather than teach you how to reproduce the pieces as shown, the directions are meant to be a starting point. We hope they will encourage your own artistic journey, guiding you as you contemplate, explore, and express your thoughts and feelings through the medium of collage. In as many cases as possible, insights into the artists' use of symbols are shared to help inspire the development of your own symbolic references. By finding images that matter to you, you'll be able to create artworks that are evocative and meaningful.

Paula Grasdal created ten of the chapter projects and each of her pieces highlights a different technique, ranging from a collaged memory box to a piece made of textured-paper tiles to a project that incorporates the ancient technique of encaustic painting. In many of her collages, you'll see a personal lexicon at work in the images of the key, the butterfly, doorways, gardens, and the dragonfly. While maintaining a recognizable personal voice, Grasdal also explores a wide range of aesthetic results and her pieces as a group will provide readers with useful insights into the workings of one artist's creative process.

A Gallery of Inspiration concludes the book with another twenty-six projects by accomplished artists that run the gamut of self-expression: a theater built into a Victorian birdcage, a photomontage inspired by Boston's "Big Dig" construction project, evocative paintings with collage elements, an elaborate metal book that pays homage to trees, and many other pieces that make the most of mixed media. The Gallery is a testament to the present-day popularity of assemblage, a three-dimensional cousin of collage in which diverse materials and found objects are joined to create a unified whole (almost half of these projects are assemblages). Along with satisfying the urge to collect neat stuff, the appeal of assemblage lies in its transformative possibilities—that the imagination of the maker can turn a handful of mundane objects into an expression of artistic inspiration.

HOLLY HARRISON

COLLAGE IS AN INTUITIVE PROCESS of concealing and revealing, adding and subtracting, until the desired result emerges from the layers. In working with a wide variety of themes, techniques, and materials for this book, I was able to push beyond my familiar methods and venture into a kind of laboratory for creativity.

If I found myself searching for inspiration, experimenting with the materials would often get me going and generate ideas. For example, while making "Silent Book" (page 12), the process of preparing paper with textures and paints influenced the direction of the artwork. I started out with a loose theme (alchemy) and specific materials (modeling paste, paper, and gold leaf), then considered the mood, colors, and overall design of the piece as I worked. An old textbook I discovered gathering dust in my studio became the backing for the collage simply because it was nearby and seemed to fit with the vision that evolved for the piece.

It was a liberating experience to stretch my boundaries and work intensely on these projects over a concentrated period. Investigating new materials and techniques sparked my imagination. Surprising, unpremeditated meanings would emerge after a project's completion, which illuminated once-hidden aspects of my memories, relationships, and dreams. These spontaneous insights paralleled the exploratory nature of making the collages and let me take more creative chances in subsequent projects.

The simple act of making a collage can lead to new possibilities. Our hope is that this book will help feed your creativity and you will soon be playing with materials and processes, and watching what develops in your own "laboratory."

PAULA GRASDAL

COLLAGE BASICS

BASIC TECHNIQUES

When working with paper, it is important to choose your adhesives carefully. Rubber cement should be avoided because over time it dries out and loses its ability to hold. Acid-free glues such as PVA will dry clear and won't stain papers as they age. Many collage artists use acrylic mediums (available in matte or gloss finish) to adhere papers because they dry clear, are easy to use, and can add translucency to light papers such as tissue or rice paper. When working with any kind of paper or board support, always coat both sides first with acrylic medium to keep the support from warping.

Many artists use acid-free papers where possible, but most found papers (newspapers, magazines, vintage papers) aren't pH-neutral. You can minimize discoloration by encasing pieces in acrylic medium, but it's likely they will still change over time. This is no reason to avoid them—found papers add character to your work and their ephemeral nature is part of their charm.

For assemblages, use industrial-strength craft glues such as E6000 for adhering heavy objects, metal, and other nonporous surfaces. And be open to alternative ways of joining materials: Transparent or masking tape, straight pins, staples, string, thread, wire, tacks, grommets, and brads are all effective and also add interesting details and textures to a piece.

BASIC COLLAGE SUPPLIES

In addition to the materials specified for each project, you'll need to have the following basic collage supplies on hand: newspapers to protect your work area, scissors (small and large), a craft knife and self-healing cutting mat, brayer, metal ruler, pencil and eraser, artist's and foam paintbrushes in assorted sizes, water jar, paint palette, and a hair dryer (for cutting drying time). Susan Pickering Rothamel, author of *The Art of Paper Collage*, recommends using a viewfinder—an empty picture-framing mat—to aid in the composition of your piece.

Most of the projects require access to photocopiers and several entail computers and black-and-white or color printers. We assume people will have the following common household items on hand: paper towels, rags, tweezers, cotton balls and swabs, rubbing alcohol, masking tape, and a stapler, as well as basic tools such as a hammer, screwdrivers, wire cutters, needle-nose pliers, and sandpaper.

GLOSSARY OF BASIC TERMS

APPLIQUÉ—To form a design or motif by sewing shaped pieces of fabric on a foundation fabric.

ASSEMBLAGE—Sculptural or three-dimensional collage that is made by assembling diverse materials and found objects.

CHINE COLLÉ—A process whereby thin papers are collaged onto printmaking paper during the printing process. The papers are placed on the inked plate, glue side up, with the printing paper on top. The plate and papers are then run through the press thereby both gluing and printing the papers.

COLLAGE—Artwork that is created by adhering images, materials, and ephemera onto a surface.

ENCAUSTIC—An ancient technique of painting with pigmented hot wax.

FROTTAGE—Taking a rubbing of a textured surface to generate a design.

GESSO—A mixture of plaster and glue or size that is used as a background for paintings (or in sculpture).

GOUACHE—An opaque, matte water-based paint.

LAUAN—¼" (½ cm) plywood veneer, often used as a support for encaustic.

MONOPRINT—A print made from a painted printing plate with elements such as texture or imagery repeated in successive prints. Each print is unique because it is painted in varying ways each time it is printed.

MONOTYPE—A print made from a painted Plexiglas plate to produce a one-of-a-kind image.

MONTAGE—The technique of assembling, overlaying, and overlapping many different materials to create an image or artwork.

PHOTOMONTAGE—The technique of combining several photographs or parts of photographs to create a composite picture or artwork.

PHOTO TRANSFER—A process by which an image is transferred from a photocopy to another surface using solvent, acrylic medium, or transfer paper.

PVA GLUE—Polyvinyl acetate; an archival adhesive that is transparent when dry and is excellent for working with papers of varied weights and textures.

VELLUM—Refers to the translucent vellum papers available in many colors and patterns in art supply stores.

Chapter One

⊚ EXPLORING ⊚
CREATIVITY

THERE ARE A FEW THINGS ABOUT COLLAGE that are unique to it as an expressive medium. One of the most obvious—and gratifying to many—is that you don't have to be able to draw to make a good collage. (In fact, one of the most famous collage artists, Joseph Cornell, never learned to draw.) This isn't to say that many collage artists aren't also excellent draftspeople; a number of the artists in this book combine their work with painting and drawing to beautiful effect. But if you're self-conscious about your drawing skills—or maybe you don't have room in your house for a studio setup—it's great to know that there's a way to make art that can be as simple as tearing up an old magazine and pasting together the images to say something new.

Artistry in collage can have multiple moments of inspiration. One of these has to do with creative collecting. Quite different from collecting baseball cards or McCoy vases, creative collecting is the searching out of interesting objects for possible use in making art. "Broken Melody" (page 16) by Judi Riesch is a perfect example of what can result when a collector has an eye for the latent magic of castoffs. The focal point of her assembled piece is a vintage photo album she unearthed at a flea market. What made the album remarkable to Riesch is that it contained a music box inside its cover, so she exposed the guts and embellished them with strung wire and wax drippings to draw attention to their distinctiveness. Though as an album the item had outlived its usefulness, Riesch recognized the beauty

inherent in the object and created an artwork around it, giving it new meaning and worth.

What Riesch experienced when she saw the album's potential is a moment of recognition that is another example of the creative inspiration fundamental to collage making. Whether wandering through a flea market or just sifting through boxes of collected ephemera while working, the artist will suddenly see an item as right—the right shape, the right statement, the right fit. Deborah Putnoi's work depends on her ability to make these recognitions. For "Enmeshed" (page 24), she let the materials inspire her, using items as diverse as pieces of embroidery, etched metal plates, and torn up drawings made specifically to use as collage elements. Working within a grid structure, she moved around the various elements and layered some sections with paint until she found a composition that worked. Her process is an intuitive one, developed over years of working as an artist. Open-ended meanings, multiple statements, and surprising combinations are all part of the creative mix in her work that makes it so evocative.

When a collage is finished, a transformation has occurred: Where there once was a random collection of found or created objects and images, there is now a cohesive whole. This creation is something more than the sum of its disparate parts and is able to express a theme or meaning that none of its components conveys alone. Chantale Légaré's "Crossings" (page 21) is a house-shaped structure, colorfully painted, embellished with beads and etching, and filled with evocative imagery. With its *mendhi*-painted foot, map fragments, and diverse found objects, the box delights in all things connected to travel and discovery. But as a whole, it is a shrine to the creative process. Through use of a vivid palette, close attention to detail, and a keen appreciation of her materials, Légaré celebrates the creative journey that takes the artist to known and unknown places, wherever they may be.

As you express your own creativity, something to consider is the way in which images resonate for you. If you find yourself repeatedly drawn to certain objects and images, these might be the beginnings of a personal vocabulary. Even working with already established systems of symbols can be a useful tool in sparking ideas. For "Silent Book" (page 12), Paula Grasdal relied on images gleaned from alchemy. Though this is imagery anyone has access to, filtering it through her own particular artistic sensibility allowed her to create a personal vision that can still be decoded by anyone with a knowledge of alchemy. Furthermore, there's something essential about the images that translates, even when the "real" meaning is missed. A viewer might not understand that the "crown of perfection" has alchemical significance, but certainly there are cultural associations with crowns that have to do with royalty, leadership, and honor. Along with any other meanings, the outspread golden wings evoke a sense of freedom and flight.

Whatever your status as artist—whether you are just starting out or are a seasoned pro—collage is a medium that will stimulate your imagination and help you to expand your artistic vision. Its reliance on creative juxtapositions of objects and images, combined with how easily it includes the creative tools from other mediums, gives it a versatility that offers the maker a wide range of creative expression. As you integrate items, objects, or images into the collage, the artistic choices you make are a function of the creative soul at work.

❧ SILENT BOOK ❧

This altered book collage was made using
textured tiles prepared by pressing found objects
onto paper covered in modeling paste. To create
a system of symbols, Paula Grasdal adapted
images taken from alchemy, the medieval pursuit
of the transmutation of base metals into gold
and the transformation of the spiritual self.
The gold-leafed heraldic crown or "crown of
perfection" represents the unification of opposites
while the wings allude to the upward flight of the
spirit and the process of elements transforming in
the alchemical vessel. The diptych format and
contrasting colors emphasize the duality in
alchemy and the coming together of opposites.

Dimensions: 9 ½" × 13" (24 cm × 33 cm) | Artist: Paula Grasdal

STEPS

1. Using PVA, cover the inside of an old book with the wrinkled paper. Coat the inside and outside of the book with gesso, let dry, and then paint as desired with acrylics.

2. Cut rag paper into several small strips and two larger pieces. Spread a thin layer of modeling paste on some of the papers with a palette knife, and then press textured objects such as leaves, stencils, fabric, art stamps or screening into the wet paste. Spread acrylic medium on the remaining strips, creating textures with the palette knife. When the papers are dry, paint them with washes of acrylic paints and highlight the textures by dry-brushing gesso or rubbing oil pastels on the raised areas.

3. Crease and then rip the prepared strips into squares. Using fabric glue, collage them to the inside of the book, making sure to balance colors and textures on each side. To create a diptych effect, leave the inside spine uncovered. Cut out arch shapes (or other framing shapes) from the larger textured papers and glue in place.

4. Decide on a system of symbols—any theme will work with this project so the possible approaches are limitless. Draw motifs on rag paper and cut out. Apply gold-leaf sizing to the cutout shapes, selected areas of the collage, and the inside of the spine. When the sizing is tacky, apply the imitation gold leaf, removing excess leaf with a soft artist's brush. After the sizing has set, lightly burnish the gold leaf with a cotton ball. Attach the gold motifs to the collage with fabric glue. Block-print a design with brown and gold acrylics down the length of the spine.

VARIATIONS

Instead of small pieces of paper, try texturing two larger sheets with the modeling paste or substitute found objects for the cutout paper motifs.

MATERIALS

- ⑤ old book cover
- ⑤ rag paper (such as watercolor or printmaking papers)
- ⑤ medium-weight wrinkled paper
- ⑤ motifs of your choice
- ⑤ modeling paste
- ⑤ gesso
- ⑤ acrylic paints
- ⑤ oil pastels
- ⑤ imitation gold leaf
- ⑤ palette knife
- ⑤ carved eraser (for block-printed design)
- ⑤ adhesives: acrylic gel medium, fabric glue (such as Sobo), diluted PVA, leaf sizing
- ⑤ basic collage supplies (see page 8)

⟲⟳ BROKEN MELODY ⟳⟲

*Like many collage artists, Judi Riesch often finds
inspiration in a single object. Here, it was the
discarded back of a vintage music-box photo
album she discovered at a flea market. She found
its mechanical inner workings unusual and
beautiful, and decided to create a loose narrative
inside the album using an old photograph,
antique textile fragments, and words and
numbers cut from vintage papers. To house the
album, she created an intimate interior space by
collaging a shadow box frame with vintage ledger
pages and sheet music. A decorative gold frame
lends the piece a Victorian feel, yet her use of
wire embellishments and beeswax drippings is
distinctively modern.*

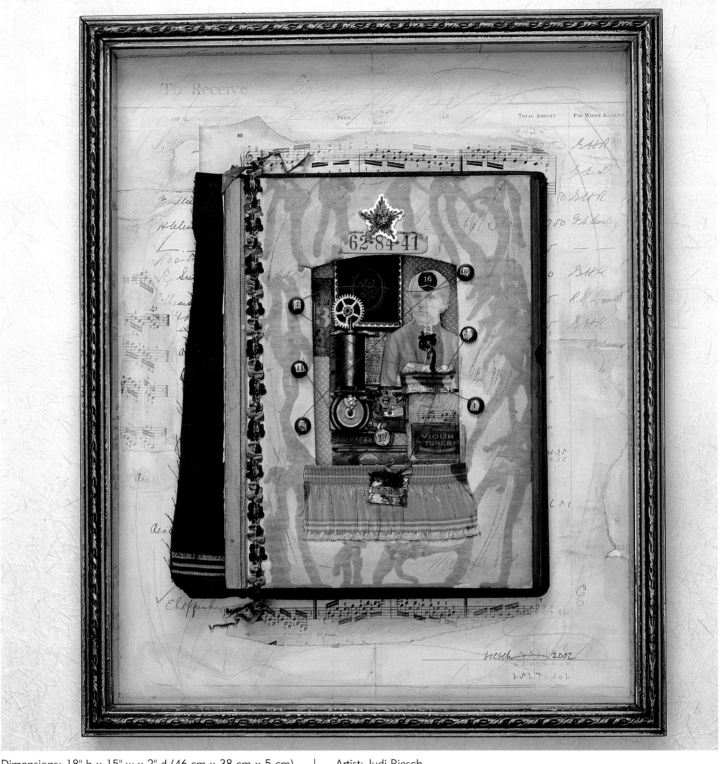

Dimensions: 18" h × 15" w × 2" d (46 cm × 38 cm × 5 cm) | Artist: Judi Riesch

BROKEN MELODY ◎

STEPS	MATERIALS

STEPS

1. Start by finding or making something special to use as the heart of your assemblage. Expose the guts of an old clock or telephone or take several interesting old items and join them together. Once you have your center, find or make a shadow box frame.

2. Cut a piece of heavy mat board to fit in the shadow box. Collage vintage papers onto the mat board using acrylic medium and cover the insides of the frame as well. Add details or washes of color, as desired, with colored pencils and acrylic paints.

3. Wire or glue the back of your centerpiece to the board. Build up the assemblage by adhering found objects, ribbons, and trim around the centerpiece (and within its workings if appropriate). Take as much time as you need—hours or even days—to move and reposition objects before adhering them. Finding the perfect arrangement is a combination of association, color, texture, and discovery.

4. To draw attention to what's being contained within, the artist stuck upholstery tacks along two sides of the opening in the album and strung wire across it. Another detail: She applied melted beeswax to the area around the opening with a small brush, which she then incised with a sharp point and rubbed with acrylic paint. Experiment freely with your materials to add textures and color until the piece feels complete.

5. Once you are satisfied, fit the entire base into the shadow box frame. Attach a wire or a saw-tooth hanger for hanging.

MATERIALS

- ◎ found object or objects for center of assemblage
- ◎ shadow box frame
- ◎ heavy mat board
- ◎ assorted vintage ribbons and trims
- ◎ vintage papers
- ◎ acrylic paints
- ◎ colored pencils
- ◎ beeswax
- ◎ stencils
- ◎ wire
- ◎ brass upholstery tacks
- ◎ adhesives: acrylic gel medium, glue, adhesive caulk
- ◎ basic collage supplies (see page 8)

◎ Judi Riesch's Creativity Tips

As a collector and keeper of fragments from the past, I find myself using these objects as a continuing source of ideas and inspiration. When creativity is challenged, I have only to look at the things I love. Something will spark an idea, a memory, often surprising me as it unfolds and takes on a new life. My involvement with this music box stemmed from a memory of one my grandmother gave me when I was a child—a tiny ballerina twirling inside a glass dome to the "Vienna Life Waltz."

ෙ TEMPLE ෙ

To get the right materials for this paper-pulp collage, which emulates the look of an ancient relic or temple, Paula Grasdal made them herself. She created a set of cast handmade papers and used diversely textured objects to add relief textures to the wet paper pulp. Once the papers were dry, she transformed them with acrylic paints and oil pastels, arranged them in a composition, and then glued them together. Though working with fragile, almost transitory materials, Grasdal has established a sense of timelessness by emphasizing the tactile nature of the materials and using a palette that evokes earth, sky, and water.

Dimensions: 13" × 12" (33 cm × 30 cm) | Artist: Paula Grasdal

TEMPLE ⏃

1. Tear the cotton linters into stamp-size pieces and soak in water for at least three hours. Place a handful of soaked linters in a blender full of water, blend until smooth, and pour the contents into a basin of tepid water. Repeat with the remaining linters, adding more water to the basin as needed. When finished, add methyl cellulose to strengthen pulp for casting.

2. Stir the pulp and water mixture, and then slide the stretched metal mesh into the basin, scooping up pulp as you lift it out. Shake the mesh gently to even out the coating of pulp on its surface. Flip the wet pulp onto a piece of felt, pressing a sponge onto the back of the mesh to help release it.

3. To cast the paper, carefully flip the damp pulp sheet off its felt backing onto a textured surface and gently press the paper into the recessed areas. Reinforce the pulp with another sheet of damp pulp if necessary. Repeat with various textured surfaces until you have at least ten embossed sheets (you can also add botanical elements such as petals, herbs, and leaves to the pulp for a beautiful effect). Leave to dry; this can take about three days but will go faster if the sheets are placed near a heat source or out in the sun.

4. When the papers are dry, gently pry them loose from the textured objects. Paint with acrylic paints, and then highlight raised areas with metallic paints or oil pastels.

5. Arrange the painted papers together to create a temple or other shape and adhere with PVA glue.

TIPS

To create handmade paper forms, cut the metal mesh into shapes (such as an arch) and use without a frame to scoop up the pulp. As an alternative to painting the dry papers, you can color the pulp in the basin with paper dyes, but you will need to use several separate basins for this method.

MATERIALS

- ⏃ three sheets of cotton linters for making pulp
- ⏃ papermaking felts or disposable dishcloths
- ⏃ sponges
- ⏃ metal screen stretched in a frame or cut into an arch shape
- ⏃ methyl cellulose
- ⏃ acrylic and metallic paints
- ⏃ oil pastels
- ⏃ objects with textured surfaces for casting (the artist used carved wood blocks, burlap fabric, and embossed tin)
- ⏃ square basin
- ⏃ blender
- ⏃ adhesive: PVA glue
- ⏃ basic collage supplies (see page 8)

CROSSINGS

Chantale Légaré's multi-media assemblage combines painted images with map fragments and found objects to comment on how the places we grow up in or travel to can shape who we are and how we think. The house shape represents a starting point or home, a place in which living, dreaming, and remembering can occur. Légaré uses a paint palette of vibrant colors reminiscent of Indian textiles, a notion that's reinforced by the image of a foot covered with mendhi patterns. Roads and rivers cut from maps lead away from the painted foot, symbolizing the many pathways walked.

Dimensions: 13 ¼" h × 10" w × 3" d (33½ cm × 25 cm × 8 cm) | Artist: Chantale Légaré

STEPS

1. Build or find a small wooden house that opens from the back. Cut a piece of glass to fit inside the front; add frosted designs using glass-etching solution, contact paper cut into stencils, and a brush. Rinse the glass thoroughly and set aside. Sand and paint the house as desired. Affix the glass inside the front with a small narrow molding just like a frame.

2. Cut a piece of lauan to fit inside the box. Add collage elements that say something about the place you are commemorating. The artist used painted architectural moldings, brass bells, and a rectangle painting she made of a small foot decorated with Indian *mendhi* patterns over fragments cut from maps of places important to her. (When she travels, the artist collects materials and artifacts to use in her work.)

3. To decorate with beads, drill holes along the box's sides. String glass beads on fishing line and attach them through the holes.

4. Seal the final collage inside the house with brackets and another piece of lauan placed behind the work. Attach an eyehook and wire for hanging.

TIPS

If another idea occurs to you while working and it's too late to make a change, write it down and save it for another piece. If you find you are "painting" too much, cut out holes to make small windows of tranquility in the work. You can use those cutouts later in other projects.

MATERIALS

- 3¾" × 48" (9½ cm × 122 cm) birch plywood, ½" (1 cm) thick
- two pieces 12" × 7¼" (30 cm × 18½ cm) lauan
- wood molding
- glass, glasscutter, and gloves
- glass-etching solution and contact paper
- acrylic paints in various colors
- embellishments such as brass bells, bits of maps, glass beads
- fishing line
- screws and nails
- brackets
- eyehook and wire
- handsaw
- miter saw
- handheld drill
- nail gun or hammer
- adhesives: acrylic gel medium, wood glue
- basic collage supplies (see page 8)

☺ Chantale Légaré's Creativity Tips

I look at my travel photo albums, art journals filled with my ideas, and old work. I always keep notes of things to do or make when I have time. I look at great masterpieces and try to figure out why they still work. At the library, I read *National Geographic* magazine to learn about other peoples and customs, textiles, and patterns. When I have a creative block, I go for a walk or work in the garden, where my hands can be creative while my mind is finding some peace.

ℰℰ ENMESHED ℰℰ

Deborah Putnoi created this colorful collaged box using a grid pattern as her organizing principle. She collected images (often her own work that she tears up to use as collage fragments), texts, fabric swatches, monoprints, and etched metal plates, then adhered them randomly, reflecting the randomness of life and creating a kind of sensory bombardment. In her work, disparate fragments and seemingly unrelated images— a sketched sheep, a painted portrait, the letter W—coexist within the loose grid much as multiple events coexist within a single moment in time. Putnoi believes her work is not complete until there is a viewer: someone who takes the assembled elements and constructs their own meaning based on personal associations and history.

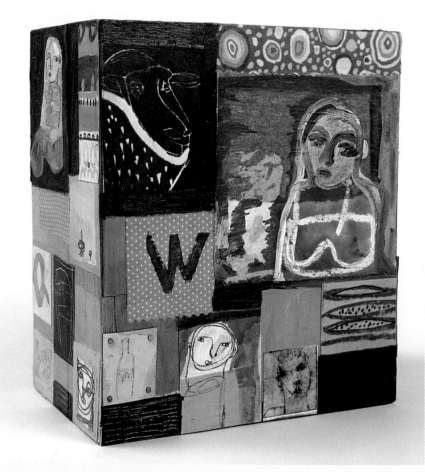

Dimensions: 9" h × 8" w × 5" d (23 cm × 20 cm × 13 cm) | Artist: Deborah Putnoi

ENMESHED ◎

STEPS

1. Gesso a wooden box, etching images into the wet gesso with a stylus. Let dry.

2. While the gesso dries, use various sized brushes and rollers to paint assorted papers that you will cut up and use in the collage. (See the Creativity Tips box for more ideas for making collage materials.)

3. Push acrylic paint or oil sticks into the incised dry gesso and wipe away excess.

4. Gather collage materials such as painted papers, old drawings, fabric, phone book pages, cardboard, old prints, etc. Start arranging the elements on the front of the box. This piece uses a basic grid format, which allows for free expression within a simple structure. Work with the grid, or experiment with other forms. Don't plan things too much and work intuitively. Take chances—you can always paint over what doesn't work. Use acrylic medium to adhere the collage materials to the box. (Tip: Acrylic medium comes in gloss or matte finish; experiment with both and use what works best for your piece.)

5. Paint the spaces around the collage elements to add another dimension. Finish by painting and collaging the sides and top of the box.

MATERIALS

◎ wooden box

◎ old drawings, prints, texts from books or journals, handpainted collage papers

◎ fabric

◎ gesso

◎ acrylic paint

◎ oil sticks

◎ stylus

◎ adhesive: acrylic gel medium

◎ basic collage supplies (see page 8)

◎ Deborah Putnoi's Creativity Tips

Do twenty one-minute drawings of your face, then rip up the pieces when you're done and create a collage from these elements. Do two-handed drawings: Draw whatever comes into your head using both hands concurrently. Let your hands keep moving. Do this exercise a few times and watch what develops. Put music on, get some tempera paint, thick brushes, and newsprint. Close your eyes and paint to the music. When the paintings are dry, rip them up and use them as collage materials.

THE CREATIVE PROCESS

DEBORAH PUTNOI

Ripping a drawing in half, a corner catches my eye, a finely drawn face of a boy next to a splash of red paint. I find an old monoprint and cut a square from it. I place the torn and cut fragments on a wooden surface, rearranging them until a composition reveals itself. I grab an old aluminum plate with an etching of a hand on it, nail it onto the surface, and glue a section of black fabric next to it. Then I take my brush, fill it with a wad of gesso, and paint the wood. Into this wet layer, I etch a drawing of a cell dividing in mitosis. Once it's dry, I rub paint into the grooves of the drawing, adding another texture. I am intrigued by the juxtaposition not only of random images but also of a multiplicity of textures and materials. My world is ripe with an abundance of images, elements, ideas, and materials—and my work attempts to capture this infinite array.

Where does the creative impulse come from? My brain, my soul, my hands embedded in the materials, the motion of making something? For me, the act of creation is a letting go. Jumping into "the unknown," I hold my breath hoping that something powerful will form out of the chatter in my mind. As I navigate my way, fragments of paper and fabric, tin and canvas surround my work-space until finally, in the mess, I discover the clarity that is the final composition.

My creative process is powered by the ability to take chances and allow randomness to exist within a formal grid structure. Usually, I work on many art pieces at one time, moving fragments from one to the next until I sense that an element works in a specific piece. I never sketch things out ahead of time and I thrive on seeing what unfolds spontaneously. I will draw a variety of images on different types of paper (phone books, tracing paper, graph paper). I will also experiment with a wide range of materials (oil stick, watercolor, tempera paint, silkscreen, potato prints) on larger pieces of paper, making abstract pieces I know I will cut up and use as fragments later. In my studio, I have a giant drawer that houses old drawings, monoprints, silkscreens, works on paper, sketches, fabric, and etching plates. As I work, I sift through my old discards and remember creating each one. Reusing them allows me to witness the regeneration of different themes and ideas in my work over time.

When I think critically about my process, I realize there are some core elements that fuel my creativity: courage, discipline, and passion. Creating something takes courage and confidence. Taking that leap into the unknown each time we create something new is a coura-geous act. When I go to the studio, I try to start working before I can think about it, because once my mind gets too involved I start to question and control every move I make. It's like plunging into the lake at the beginning of summer. If I slowly inch my way in and feel the water a little bit at a time, I may decide that it's too cold and I won't go in at all. But when I just jump in, I realize that the experience is exhilarating and the water feels great.

One reason people often hold back is a fear of making mistakes. But the idea of "mistakes" is almost not valid: A mistake is an unforeseen opportunity. It is a way to gen-erate previously unimagined ideas and to find and create new possibilities. Sometimes I will draw with my left hand to purposely make mistakes or to make my drawing more eccentric. I search out the uninvited marks or disturbing color to see how that will add an element of surprise to the composition. As Shaun McNiff says in his book *Trust the Process: An Artist's Guide to Letting Go*, "In the creative process, one action leads to another, and the final outcome is shaped by a chain of expressions that could never be planned in advance." Openness to mistakes, mess, chaos, and the unknown all allow the process to flow and unfold.

At the same time, discipline is essential. Having an idea that you would like to make something is only the first step. Getting in there and doing it, and continuing to do it, is almost the most important aspect of creativity. It's about going to the "office"—be it the studio, the cafe, the outdoors—and working. For me, at times, this is the hardest part of being an artist. It is difficult to face work that is not progressing and there are times I just don't "feel" creative. But the discipline of holding to a set studio time, of going there and making something (anything), is important in keeping the creative process dynamic.

Finally, involvement in the creative process requires passion for the whole endeavor. I need to rip paper and collage the torn shreds onto a white canvas. I need to feel the paint sliding over the textured surface, to thrust my brush into the heart of the composition. I crave the feeling of my materials. I love to mix colors and watch the subtle ways they can change by just the slightest addition or subtraction of another color. I had a teacher at art school who said to a fellow student, "If it is a choice to paint, then don't choose it. Painting chooses you—it is an inexplicable need."

For each person the creative process is a unique exploration. Each of us has an individual fingerprint and the way we work in expressing ourselves is also singular. As I place the final element into the composition, I step back and look at the piece as a whole. I start to make connections among the shapes and forms, and in my mind's eye I glimpse another way the work could be resolved. I grab another canvas, pick up an old drawing and cut out a section, collage it onto the surface, and I am off creating the next piece—one in a chain of pieces that I make as an outgrowth of the creative process, which is central to my existence.

 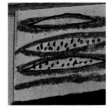  

Chapter Two

CHRONICLING RELATIONSHIPS

THE CONNECTIONS BETWEEN and among people, and between people and the world they live in, are the subject of the following chapter. With these projects, the artists seek to honor special relationships in their lives and to divine the meaning of connectedness and relating. Projects range from personal portraits of a specific loved one to overviews of how identity is affected by the societal rules and expectations that shape human relations.

Although the personal nature of some of these works makes them seemingly less accessible to the viewer, who likely will not know particular details, their atmosphere of intimacy serves to draw the viewer in, allowing a more intuitive understanding to occur. In "The Chess Lesson" (page 36), Paula Grasdal put together an affectionate portrait of her father that reflects his love of his profession—teaching math and physics—and of chess. Because we know the game requires two players, the presence of the artist is implied as that second player, the recipient of the lesson. Encountering the board head on, the viewer experiences the piece from the artist's perspective, that is, "across the chess board" from the father. And even though the youthful man looking back at us is a stranger, we experience him in the role of father by bringing our own memories and feelings about our fathers to the piece. In this way, a particularly private vision becomes universally accessible.

While some artists choose a subtly implied presence (or aren't present at all) in their collages, many others successfully place themselves inside a piece, granting further insight into the story of a relationship by spelling out their place within it. Maria G. Keehan uses a photograph of herself looking up at representations of memories and stories about her grandmothers, in "What I Think I Know About Elizabeth and Maggie" (page 39), to show how she is seeking to know them and how half of her comes from each of them. Meredith Hamilton ("Le Mariage," page 42) uses an image of herself as a princess bride (a playful nod to notions of fairytale romance) on top of a wedding cake carousel, which represents relationships as filtered through the lens of marriage. Her knight wears shining armor with a twist: He sports a literal "blockhead."

Taking on the theme of a relationship to a place rather than a person, Grasdal's "Pond Life" (page 30) honors an island along the Pacific Northwest Coast where she spent time as a child. Nestling a portrait of lily pads among repeated images of the pond's lush surface and encasing the whole in layers of colorful encaustic paints, the artist built an abstraction of water and plant life that evokes rather than re-creates the actual pond. The only visitor is a dragonfly, hovering in place over the blue water. A symbol of regeneration and change, the dragonfly represents the biological cycles in the real pond and also changes to the pond as it exists in the memory of the artist.

Objects and images within an assemblage or collage can carry meanings according to where they are positioned in a piece. Hamilton's wedding cake collage uses the tiers of the cake to establish a social structure wherein the married couple is the center, their children are the second tier, and friends, career, financial decisions, and home make up the final group of forces at play in the couple's life. Another artist's collage of the same subject could look very different if, for example, there were no children and so career or friends played a larger role. In Keehan's piece, the placement of images and objects hints at discrete narratives within the whole: At the center of each half is the grandmother whose life is featured; the background is their actual "background" (photos of their birthplace); and surrounding details tell of journeys (a ship at sea, a map of destinations, parts of a diary) and religious faith (a rosary, an image of the Virgin Mary).

The choices you make about how to approach your subject will greatly affect the outcome, so take time when you're getting started to think about what you want to say. When working on a place collage, think about what aspects of the place are most meaningful to you. Consider various times of day and photographs taken under different weather conditions. What mood do they establish? Which ones best represent how you feel about the place? If

people are a part of the appeal, include them. Grasdal focused on a pond in her place collage, but Bowen Island also has beautiful forests and beaches she could have highlighted for dramatically different results. A series of three or four collages could show the island's varied topography and offers an interesting alternative approach.

When chronicling a relationship with a person, consider it from a variety of angles: Do you want to portray a relationship as it is (or was) or an idealized vision of what you wish for it? What details and images will offer insight into the personalities of the people in your collage? And where are you—a part of the story or, like the viewer, outside of it? The key is to follow your instincts, letting the collage develop with each new addition or change. And nothing says you have to focus outward: A relationship collage can also offer a way to examine aspects of your own personality and life, allowing you to explore your relationship to yourself. Whatever your approach, as you are positioning images, textures, and objects in layer after layer, you'll find yourself engaged in an intuitive process that may begin with a specific idea but will undoubtedly lead to a discovery of much more.

꩜ POND LIFE ꩜

This lushly hued piece, encaustic and collage on plywood, celebrates the artist's relationship to a special place—Bowen Island, located on the Pacific Northwest Coast. Recalling childhood explorations of the island's natural wonders, Paula Grasdal focused on images of a pond, carpeted with lily pads and whirring with iridescent dragonflies. The combined elements of photocopied photographs, incised drawing, and translucent wax create a tactile layered effect characteristic of the encaustic technique.

The repeated lily pad image and the translucent blues and greens of the encaustic paints lend the piece tranquility, evoking thoughts of quiet contemplation and feeling connected to the natural world.

Dimensions: 13" × 10¾" (33 cm × 27½ cm) | Artist: Paula Grasdal

POND LIFE ☺

1. To begin this project, read about encaustic technique on page 45. Make multiple photocopies of various photographs of a place that is meaningful to you. Enlarge or shrink them to vary the composition. To create the background design, arrange the photocopies in a repeat pattern on plywood and trim them to fit. Glue the background papers in place with PVA, roll with a brayer, and let dry. Reserve the main image for use in Step 3.

2. Paint a layer of hot encaustic medium over the collaged papers and the board's edges. Blend pre-mixed encaustic colors with encaustic medium for a translucent effect, and paint the tinted wax onto the first wax layer. Fuse the layers together with a heat gun.

3. Apply the main image by heating a section of the wax background with a heat gun and pressing the paper onto this heated area. Encapsulate the paper by painting hot wax medium over its surface. Fuse with a heat gun.

4. Cut out selected shapes from your photocopies (the artist chose lily pads) and collage these on top of the main image and elsewhere on the composition, using the same method as in Step 3. You can also use pressed leaves, old letters, maps, etc. Engrave an image with a stylus into the wax (such as the dragonfly) and rub an oil pastel over the incised lines. Wipe away the excess pastel with a linseed-oil-soaked cloth.

5. Create a border by painting opaque wax in a contrasting color around the board's edges and sides. Fuse with a heat gun and let cool. To create a surface sheen, polish the wax with a soft cloth.

MATERIALS

- ☺ black-and-white or color photocopies of photographs
- ☺ piece of 3/4" (2 cm) plywood for backing
- ☺ oil pastels
- ☺ linseed oil
- ☺ encaustic paints and medium
- ☺ heated palette (for heating wax)
- ☺ heat gun with variable speeds
- ☺ natural bristle brushes
- ☺ stylus
- ☺ adhesive: PVA glue
- ☺ basic collage supplies (see page 8)

TIPS

Wax is not compatible with acrylics (including acrylic gesso) but can be combined or layered with oil paints and oil sticks. To clean your brushes, dip them in a tin of hot paraffin and wipe the bristles with paper towels.

❧ 4 DRESSES ❧

Dresses are metaphorically laden with meaning about feminine identity, from issues related to physical appearance to expectations about women's roles and relationships. To suggest how societal forces shape women from childhood onward, Jane Maxwell uses a repeated paper doll-dress form as her central image. She manipulates the images with colorful vellums and photocopied imagery, then layers them over various found papers such as texts, sewing patterns, and printed images. Despite the rigorousness of the dress form and its insistence on conformity, individual "personalities" are visible through the vellum and successfully subvert the form.

Dimensions: 5½" × 15" (14 cm × 38 cm) | Artist: Jane Maxwell

4 DRESSES ◎

STEPS

1. Select imagery from a variety of sources—magazines, books, found papers. Seek out imagery that relates to an overall message, for example, "4 Dresses" features writing from sewing patterns and related circle imagery, representing the whole person beneath the cutout form.

2. Photocopy chosen images onto vellum in various colors. Play around with varying image size, using color and black-and-white copies, and combining or layering images right on the copy machine. Another good layering material is clear acetate, which photocopies well and offers a slick contrasting texture.

3. Find a central image to repeat (in this case, an actual doll-dress form) or create your own. Choose something that speaks to you—a tree, a window, a tiara. Repeated imagery will have impact in a line of two, three, or four, and also two over two.

4. Build repeating forms by layering found papers under and over the central image and by utilizing negative spaces. Create dimension and contrast with acrylic paint or charcoal.

5. Join the repeated images using a variety of binding materials (tape, stitching, glue). Be creative: Household items such as straight pins, masking tape, and staples add texture and interest.

MATERIALS

- ◎ vellum, clear and assorted colors
- ◎ background imagery from books, postcards, sewing patterns
- ◎ photocopies of various images
- ◎ acrylic paints
- ◎ charcoal pencil
- ◎ thread and sewing machine
- ◎ adhesive: PVA glue
- ◎ basic collage supplies (see page 8)

◎ Jane Maxwell's Creativity Tips

Don't limit yourself to solid colored papers: Transparent vellum and acetate papers are also available in a variety of patterns and become high-impact layering pieces when transformed by a photocopied image. Another tip: Take a pre-existing piece of your art, place it on a copy machine, and transfer it onto a variety of papers. It's a great starting point for future pieces. And keep your eyes open for unique paper and images. Flea markets and antiques malls are great for digging up vintage signs, posters, books, ledgers, etc. Old papers have a special color and textural quality that adds depth, richness, and history to a collage.

⊙⊂ THE CHESS LESSON ⊃⊙

This richly colored fabric collage pays homage to the artist's father, a physics and math teacher and an avid chess player. Paula Grasdal used photo transfer techniques to create the portrait of her father as a young man and the silhouettes of chess pieces. Transferred images of physics equations evoke a classroom blackboard and together with pieces of metallic mesh build a containing border for the chessboard. The board's grid pattern organizes the disparate elements of the piece and also reflects her father's logical and thoughtful approach to life.

Dimensions: 12" × 12" (30 cm × 30 cm) | Artist: Paula Grasdal

THE CHESS LESSON ◎

STEPS

1. To transfer a photocopy of a portrait, brush a small piece of canvas and the photocopy with acrylic matte medium, and place the image face down on the coated fabric. Press out air bubbles and let dry thoroughly (about 24 hours). Soak the canvas in warm water and gently rub off the paper until the image is exposed (it will be reversed). Let dry, then tint the portrait with diluted acrylic paints.

2. Cut white silk organza pieces and other collage elements for the border. Transfer desired images using the technique described on page 85. Tint the organza with diluted silk paints, let dry, and set with an iron.

3. Choose a base pattern or design that says something about the person or relationship in your collage. To make a chessboard pattern, draw a grid on a 12" × 12" (30 cm × 30 cm) piece of canvas, leaving a 2" (5 cm) border. Paint the checkerboard pattern and border with acrylics in colors of your choice. When dry, iron the fabric on the unpainted side to flatten.

4. Make or buy a stencil for the border design and stencil the design using metallic acrylic paint. Let dry.

5. Brush fabric glue onto the canvas border and adhere the organza photo transfers made in Step 2. Apply other decorative fabrics where desired. Embellish the portrait (the artist used fragments of a photocopy on acetate and some metallic organza) and adhere it to the composition. As a finishing touch, glue on found metal objects using the industrial-strength glue.

VARIATIONS

Add hand or machine embroidery as another layer of embellishment. Areas of fabric can also be stitched and then cut away to reveal contrasting fabrics underneath (this is called reverse-appliqué; see "Relic IV" on page 120).

MATERIALS

- ◎ canvas
- ◎ silk organza or other natural fiber cloth, in white and metallic gold
- ◎ fiberglass mesh
- ◎ found objects for embellishments
- ◎ photocopies of photographs and other design elements
- ◎ images (such as chess pieces) photo-copied on clear acetate
- ◎ decorative stencil for border design
- ◎ stencil brush
- ◎ acrylic paints
- ◎ fabric or silk paints
- ◎ acrylic matte medium and oil of wintergreen (for transferring images)
- ◎ burnishing tool
- ◎ adhesives: fabric glue, industrial-strength craft glue
- ◎ basic collage supplies (see page 8)

❦ WHAT I THINK I KNOW ❦ ABOUT ELIZABETH AND MAGGIE

Maria G. Keehan set out to make this multi-media collage about her grandmothers by limiting herself solely to what she remembered from family lore rather than validating those memories by making inquiries. Using a silverware case as her container, she dedicated one side to each grandmother and filled it with ephemera that recalled stories or images she associated with each: a rosary, pieces of china, and a portrait of Rudolph Valentino for Elizabeth; some old buttons, scraps from a travel diary, and photos of the coal mining town where she grew up for Maggie. With dreamlike imagery, multiple layers, and colorful found objects, Keehan evokes an intimate vision of her family heritage.

Dimensions: 14" h × 22" w × 2½" d (36 cm × 56 cm × 6 cm) | Artist: Maria G. Keehan

WHAT I THINK I KNOW ABOUT ELIZABETH AND MAGGIE ☺

STEPS

1. Find a suitable container: an old silverware case, wooden cigar box, painted metal tin. Clean up the insides and paint with gold-leaf paint. Cover hot-press illustration board with marbleized or other paper and glue it into the back of your box.

2. Assemble photographs and found images. Choose a portrait and have an iris print or color photocopy made to size. Using acrylic medium, mount it on Bristol board backed with gold tissue paper. Cut out with a craft knife.

3. If you can, use a computer to alter photographs in creative ways. The artist downloaded images to Photoshop, played with them, and embellished printouts with colored pencils. She also colorized black-and-white images (of Rudolph Valentino) and created strips of small headshots of her grandmothers. Many of these effects can be reproduced manually with the help of a color photocopier.

4. Do research to find out things, such as what the town where your person was born was like and other historical facts that relate to their life, or rely on your memories alone. Copy passages from their favorite book. If possible, obtain photocopies from diaries or letters in their handwriting.

5. Assemble all of your materials (including relevant found objects) and play with arrangements in the box. Glue things down slowly, considering the composition as you work. Let pieces relate to each other to create a narrative about the person or relationship you're commemorating. Draw attention to details through interesting placement (such as the ship in the corner seen here), juxtaposition, and repetition.

MATERIALS

- ☺ case to house collage
- ☺ color printouts or photocopies of photographs and diary entries
- ☺ iris prints (high-end digital prints; color photocopies may be substituted)
- ☺ found objects and embellishments such as buttons, stamps, stones, rosary beads, old photographs
- ☺ decorative papers such as embossed tissue paper, gold tissue paper, marbleized paper
- ☺ gold-leaf paint
- ☺ colored pencil
- ☺ Bristol board and hot-press illustration board
- ☺ heavyweight rag paper
- ☺ sandpaper
- ☺ brass hinges
- ☺ friend with digital camera
- ☺ adhesives: acrylic matte medium, craft glue, wood glue
- ☺ basic collage supplies (see page 8)

☾☾ LE MARIAGE ☾☾

The conceit Meredith Hamilton created for this watercolor-based collage about marriage is a wedding cake carousel—a traditional symbol of romantic love reconfigured to reflect the realities of life, where relationships are anything but static. To build the piece, she first inked, then collaged and painted on top of handmade paper to create a unified cake shape. Next, she added stamps, images from vintage books and cards, smaller watercolors and drawings, and money fragments. The origins of the merry-go-round lie in the Crusades, and the name "carrousel" originally meant "mini war" in French. Hamilton posits that marriage, too, is a kind of mini war, with many competing forces at play. Open "doors" in the cake reveal the mechanism that powers the carousel, and the bride's hand (the hand of the artist) holds the control.

Dimensions: 19" in diameter (48 cm) | Artist: Meredith Hamilton

STEPS

1. Paint or draw an unadorned wedding cake. This will be the foundation of your collage, whether you fill it using painting and collage as the artist has done or by collaging on cutout images. Decorate the cake with washes of paint, colorful paper, found or created images, rhinestones, ribbons—whatever works for you. (The artist used pieces of maps and roses made of the leafy drawings on money.)

2. The top layer: If you are making the collage to represent your own marriage, find or make a representation of yourself and your partner. (If you aren't married, rework the image to reflect other important relationships.) This piece is topped with a bridal couple. The groom's head is a drawing of a "blockhead," a wry comment by the artist on the stolid way her husband sometimes relates to people. The bride's face is George Washington's face cut from a U.S. dollar bill and represents financial considerations in life.

3. Layer two contains a second tier of forces, in this case, children. Again, choose whatever is relevant to you—children, friends, career—and find or make appropriate images. The artist has depicted her children riding carousel animals that mirror their personalities: a phoenix, a griffin, and a Pegasus-fish. Their faces are cutout images from Victorian cards.

4. The third tier of the cake is for other significant forces or events: the purchase of a house (shown on a spring, bouncing crazily); friends (represented by animals partying in a swan boat); and career (the artist's desk, looking blank because there's never enough time for art). Alter and embellish your images in creative ways as the artist has done, to show how you feel about these elements in your life.

MATERIALS

- ☉ heavy paper for base (the artist used a handmade paper by Twinrocker)
- ☉ interesting found papers such as money fragments, old stamps, images from old books and maps
- ☉ drawings or photographs of people in your life or representations of those people (from magazines, books, vintage cards)
- ☉ watercolors
- ☉ adhesive: PVA glue
- ☉ basic collage supplies (see page 8)

ENCAUSTIC COLLAGE

PAULA GRASDAL

Encaustic is an ancient technique of painting with pigmented hot wax that produces a luminous and tactile surface. Encaustic paint has three main ingredients: purified beeswax, damar resin (a natural tree resin), and pigment. Encaustic medium, which is beeswax mixed with damar, produces translucent glazes when mixed with the pigmented wax. Encaustic can be cast, carved, scraped, scratched, and embedded with collage materials to produce a wide variety of intriguing results.

Recent availability of premixed encaustic paints and medium has inspired the reemergence of this versatile medium. Artists such as Lynne Perrella (page 51), Tracy Spadafora (page 114), and Cynthia Winika (page 118) incorporate collage elements into their encaustic paintings to great effect. The warm wax acts like an adhesive, and the artist simply encapsulates the absorbent collage materials in the wax. Paper, fabric, photos, leaves, gold leaf, and thread are just a few of the many suitable materials.

BASIC TECHNIQUES

Encaustic technique can be broken down into three basic elements: heating the pigmented wax on a hot palette, painting the hot wax onto an absorbent surface, and fusing each layer with a heat source. For heating the wax, place various colors in small tins on a hot palette (this can be purchased from R&F Handmade Paints or improvised using a Teflon griddle on a hot plate; see Product Resource Guide, page 132) and heat to no more than 220°F (104°C). Using natural bristle brushes (synthetic ones will melt), blend the colors on the hot palette and paint onto the support. Any absorbent surface—a braced wooden panel, watercolor paper, plaster, or "clayboard"—is suitable as a support for wax. Fuse each layer by reheating the wax with a heat gun or tacking iron (this step is important as wax tends to separate into discrete layers). Ventilate well with an exhaust fan next to your work surface as overheated wax fumes can be toxic. If your wax starts smoking, it is too hot—turn down the heat on your palette even if the temperature gauge is at 220°F (104°C).

COLLAGING WITH WAX

Layering delicate paper and wax creates a subtle effect of floating textures and images. Try drawing on translucent rice paper with oil pastel and then embedding it in wax: The paper will seem to disappear, leaving the drawing suspended. Many layers of wax and paper can be added to create a rich surface with lots of depth. Another technique is to cover the support with collage material before adding the encaustic.

EXTENDING THE PROCESS

There are many methods of working with encaustic; here are a few ideas for inspiration. Images can be transferred onto the wax at any stage in the layering process (and no solvents are necessary). Simply place a photocopy of an image face down on cool wax and burnish it with a bone folder. Peel off the paper to reveal a reversed image on the wax. Gilding can be added as a final stage by simply burnishing the metallic leaf with a cotton ball. To embed a line drawing in the surface, incise the wax with a stylus, rub an oil pastel into the lines, and remove excess pastel to reveal the markings. Finally, for an antique effect, layer contrasting encaustic paints on top of each other and, like an archeologist, scrape into the surface to reveal the underlying colors.

For more information on encaustic, see *The Art of Encaustic Painting* by Joanne Mattera.

Chapter Three

⊙ EXPRESSING ⊙
DREAMS AND WISHES

THERE'S SOMETHING ABOUT THE NATURE OF COLLAGE—the juxtaposing of images, the playing with scale, the use of photographically realistic depictions—that has the quality of being both real and unreal at the same time. This in part explains its popularity among the Surrealist artists of the 1930s and 1940s, whose groundbreaking works are the most widely known examples of fine art collage. It also explains why the medium lends itself so well to the exploration of dreams—not just the expression of dreamlike narratives, but the articulation of an artist's wishes and desires. The artists in this chapter do a little of both, and their creations range from concentrated works focused on a single theme to dynamic pieces whose many parts evoke myriad interconnected meanings.

In "Transformation" (page 54), Paula Grasdal explores the theme of change and mutability as expressed through the image of a butterfly, surrounded by sinuous green vines and placed against a patch of vivid sky. Abstract in the manner of a dream, in which a butterfly represents the dreamer, this evocative piece celebrates the transformative possibilities inherent in any significant life change. It also shows us that collages don't have to spell things out to effectively get their meaning across. When you're thinking about how to begin a project, be open to thematic approaches rather than getting bogged down in specific narrative details. As the modernists used to say, sometimes less truly is more.

A project that successfully waxes specific, Kathy Cano-Murillo's "World Traveler's Dream Mobile" (page 63) is a fanciful construction made of ordinary materials: CDs, paper, dowels, ribbon, and beads. A kinetic presentation of twelve miniature collages, each of which represents a country the artist would like to travel to, this intricate mobile embodies the inquisitive energy of the dreamer who wishes to explore the unknown. Pictures of elephants, dancers, drinks, and dragons decorate the vibrant disc surfaces, joining together multiple fantasies about adventure and travel. Another interesting aspect to this piece is that because it is a mobile, it actually moves—a further way to underline the fact that it is about travel and moving around in the world.

In a slightly more surreal vein, Olivia Thomas conjured up a magical doll (page 48) that houses dreams and wishes. With a body made of artfully appliquéd and painted fabric, a photo transfer face (from a vintage photograph), and crochet-hook arms, the doll seems like an amalgamation of the aesthetics of different eras. She carries simple objects in her belly—a key, a heart, coins, and dice—that symbolize her inner desires for wisdom, love, prosperity, and luck. (When making a project like this, choose objects that have special meaning, as they will add potency to the wish.) The dreamy effect of the painted fabric surface makes an effective visual foil to the everyday nature of the found objects, creating a context in which it is easy to believe in their talisman-like powers. Because of the ease with which real items can be incorporated into collages, artists can take advantage of the evocative powers of those objects to create shrine-like artworks in which everyday things can symbolize more complex desires for happiness, artistic fulfillment, or love.

Making use of a range of surrealist effects, Holly Harrison's "Dream House" (page 60) depicts specific wishes and desires for a happy life through a whimsical representation of an ideal house. Liberally sprinkling the picture with under- and oversize images, the artist shows a bird making its nest atop a red house, which has several windows open to reveal specific desires: romance, artistic friends, and fabulous shoes. The smoke curling from the chimney is computer-manipulated sheet music, while (in a nod to René Magritte) silver folk art stars sparkle in a daytime sky. Happy flowers wear human faces, a map of New York covers the roof, and game pieces mark the path to the front door. The key to making a piece like this is that there are no rules—follow your imagination wherever it leads. Just as dream logic creates fantastical scenarios

and disjointed narratives, so does this collage explore the desires of the mind and heart through impossible scale, quirky juxtapositions, and playfully altered imagery.

As demonstrated by the range of projects not just in this chapter but in the book as a whole, collage is an extremely flexible medium. And because it requires an intuitive approach—piecing things together that seem to fit, finding a composition that "feels right"—there are almost no limits to what you might discover or say. As you move your collage elements around on a surface, you'll find that some images seem to "speak" to each other while others retreat into the background, letting themselves be obscured by veils of paint or paper only to assert themselves in the finished product as secret meanings or partially revealed truths. In the same way that a dreamer moves through a dream, piecing together disparate elements until a kind of narrative is born, so does the artist travel through the making of a collage, without fully knowing where he or she is going but confident in the merits of the journey.

❦ ART DOLL ❦

Combining found objects with fabric collage,
stamping, and photo transfer techniques,
Olivia Thomas has shaped a whimsical
personification of her hopes and dreams: A red
and yellow doll with burning desires caged in her
belly, held in place by a simple mesh screen.
By embellishing layers of patterned fabric with
buttons, beads, and wire, Thomas has created a
rich, tactile surface filled with personal symbols.
She also plays with scale and visual contrasts,
combining a vintage photograph face and wiry
crochet-hook arms with a rectangular body to
produce a surrealistic effect.

Dimensions: 9¼" h × 5¾" w × 1¾" d (23½ cm × 14½ cm × 4½ cm)　|　Artist: Olivia Thomas

STEPS	MATERIALS

STEPS

1. Paint a piece of muslin, using two to three colors. Add stamp designs or designs made by applying paint with found objects. If you're having trouble starting, establish a color scheme or theme. Anything goes—don't be afraid to try any idea, no matter how outrageous it seems at first.

2. Cut out one doll shape as desired from the muslin and another from a commercial print to use as back and front. Cut out legs and arms (or make them out of found objects, see Step 4). Stuff and sew closed. Use a photo transfer for the face (for this technique, see page 85). Appliqué fabrics onto the doll shape, and add trims and laces, mixing textures and juxtaposing opposites (soft/hard, shiny/dull, etc.). If a sewing machine is not available, sew by hand.

3. Sew closed the doll torso by placing front right sides together, making sure to leave an opening for stuffing. Turn the fabric right side out, stuff with batting, and complete the seam by hand. For a rustic effect, try using rugged whipstitch embroidery.

4. Embellish the body, head, and legs with beads, sequins, wire, buttons, etc. Attach a small screen area and fill it with found objects that symbolize your heart's desires. Sew on the legs and arms. The appendages can be made out of anything you fancy; the artist used old rusted crochet hooks wrapped with wires and beads for arms.

MATERIALS

- ☺ fabrics such as muslin and a printed fabric
- ☺ photo transfer
- ☺ found objects such as a key, heart, coins, dice
- ☺ embellishments such as beads, sequins, trims, lace, buttons, screen
- ☺ stuffing
- ☺ paints
- ☺ oil of wintergreen (for transfers)
- ☺ crayons
- ☺ stamps
- ☺ objects for printing on the fabric
- ☺ pliers
- ☺ wire
- ☺ needle, thread, and sewing machine
- ☺ basic collage supplies (see page 8)

☺ Olivia Thomas's Creativity Tips

The best thing that works for me is that the more I create, the more I create. Making and creating things generates endless ideas for me to try. I keep notebooks of ideas and often refer to them for a jumpstart. I like to pick a theme (love, angst, chaos) and color scheme to get going on projects. Just choose three to five colors and go from there. Let a piece mutate often, changing as it goes, until it has a life of its own.

✺ CEREMONIAL FIGURE I ✺

To create an image with the look of an antique icon, Lynne Perrella combined collage with the ancient technique of encaustic painting. She was able to create the aged effect by building up many wax layers over images she applied to the support using photo transfer techniques. With its luminescent colors broken up by lines scratched into the surface, the piece is reminiscent of a stained-glass window on which a talismanic winged figure—a muse or perhaps the artist's creative self—is surrounded by the essential elements of its creativity.

Dimensions: 12" × 9" (30 cm × 23 cm) | Artist: Lynne Perrella

CEREMONIAL FIGURE I ⑨

STEPS

1. To begin this project, read about encaustic technique on page 45. Gather images that compel you—dream images or representations of fantasies or goals. Make black-and-white photocopies and use these to make photo transfers onto a piece of printmaking paper (for the solvent transfer technique, see page 85). Apply the transfers so they create a pattern base for the collage.

2. Glue the printmaking paper onto the masonite and weight it overnight. To prevent the first layer of paint from being absorbed into the paper, apply a thin layer of melted beeswax to the surface. Apply multiple layers of encaustic paint to build up a "history," until you are satisfied with the look.

3. Add collage elements by dipping them into encaustic medium and then placing them on the support. Burnish them with a rigid plastic scraper. Be creative in your choice of materials: The artist made the figure's torso and wings from a manila file folder. The androgynous face is an archival image she often uses; it transforms and morphs in novel ways with each new collage.

4. When the elements are all in place, scribe into the wax surface with a sharp tool. Rub dark oil sticks into the markings and wipe away excess color. In this piece, a web of scribed lines enhances the "faux icon" aspect and adds a sense of history and deterioration. You can also use this technique to add words or images that expand or comment upon your theme.

5. Once the collage is fully dry, buff the surface to bring up the warmth of the colors and add sheen.

MATERIALS

- ⑨ piece of untempered masonite
- ⑨ printmaking paper (the artist used Arches)
- ⑨ photocopies of images
- ⑨ collage elements such as vintage or handmade papers
- ⑨ oil of wintergreen (for transfers)
- ⑨ beeswax
- ⑨ encaustic paints and medium
- ⑨ oil sticks
- ⑨ natural bristle brushes
- ⑨ scribing tools
- ⑨ heated palette (for heating wax)
- ⑨ plastic scraper
- ⑨ heated spatula
- ⑨ basic collage supplies (see page 8)

⑨ Lynne Perrella's Creativity Tips

The best way to maintain a constant and lively flow of creativity is to acknowledge our lifelong enthusiasms and use them as an endless reference library. Return to colors, images, themes, quotations, and iconography that have always resonated strongly for you. The artwork done as a result of honoring those enthusiasms is bound to be personal, revealing, and reflective of our true selves.

❀ TRANSFORMATION ❀

With its subtle variations in texture and color, Paula Grasdal's ethereal printed rice paper collage gives the impression of being a moving image caught in a single moment. Grasdal achieved the effect by collaging layers of translucent, printed rice papers onto heavier, earth-toned papers, then emphasizing the wrinkled surface of the glued papers with white oil pastel. A monoprint of a butterfly, a symbol of transformation, is set against a background of sinuous growing vines. It's as if the butterfly is emerging from the tangled weeds into an open meadow under a blue sky.

Dimensions: 16" × 15" (41 cm x 38 cm) | Artist: Paula Grasdal

TRANSFORMATION ☺

STEPS

1. This project can be made using any images that inspire you, especially those drawn from nature. Draw images of your choice on sketch paper. Place a piece of Mylar film over the secondary image (in this case, the vine drawing), trace it with a pencil, and cut the shape out with a craft knife. Set aside.

2. Brush water-mixable oil paints diluted with a small amount of water-mixable linseed oil onto the Mylar shape, and place a piece of damp rice paper on top. Cover the back of the paper with a sheet of Mylar film and burnish with a wooden spoon to transfer the image. Repeat several times to create collage materials.

3. To create a monoprint of your primary image (the butterfly), place a small piece of Mylar film over the drawing and paint the image directly onto the film with diluted water-mixable oils. Place the Mylar printing plate, paint side down, on a piece of dampened rice paper, and burnish with the back of a wooden spoon. Let dry.

4. Decide on the general composition of your piece and keep it in mind as you work. Cut a piece of the brown paper to use as backing and collage rice papers to it with diluted PVA. Add layers of the printed papers made in Step 2, tearing some of the papers to create a random background design in selected areas. Let dry. (If desired, coat the surface with diluted glue to emphasize the paper's translucency.) To build up the collage, lightly brush the wrinkled surfaces with gesso; add more printed papers and also gold tissue paper. To create a colorful area like the blue square, paint a section with diluted water-mixable oils, let dry, and highlight the textures with a white oil pastel.

5. Gesso a small piece of brown paper, collage print fragments onto it, and then glue the monoprint made in Step 3 on top. Let dry, then glue into place on the collage.

6. Glue the completed collage to a canvas board cut to size and roll with a brayer to smooth out air bubbles.

MATERIALS

- ☺ images for inspiration
- ☺ medium-weight brown paper
- ☺ assorted translucent rice papers and metallic gold tissue paper
- ☺ sketch paper
- ☺ canvas board
- ☺ Mylar polyester film
- ☺ gesso
- ☺ water-mixable oil paints and water-mixable linseed oil (or substitute water-based printing inks)
- ☺ white oil pastel
- ☺ wooden spoon
- ☺ spray bottle
- ☺ two 9" × 12" (23 cm × 30 cm) pieces of Plexiglas
- ☺ adhesive: PVA glue
- ☺ basic collage supplies (see page 8)

TIPS

Vary the density and color of the paint on the secondary shape for a more interesting print (the artist used a palette of olive green, yellow ochre, and brown for the vine). To dampen the rice papers for printing, lightly mist every other sheet and press the papers between two pieces of Plexiglas.

ℰℰ ARCADIA ℰℰ

Inspired by the courtyard gardens of Persian
miniatures, Paula Grasdal created a paper
collage that embodies her vision of an idyllic
sanctuary. To make the layered background, she
collaged various rice papers onto printmaking
paper. Then she used a monoprinting process
and water–based media to embed patterns and
textures into the paper, some of which she cut
into the arch and tree shapes. The artist was able
to make this highly textured, multi–layered
collage without a printmaking press by using a
Mylar printing plate, absorbent printmaking
paper, and a burnishing tool.

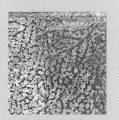

Dimensions: 12 ½" × 9" (32 cm × 23 cm) | Artist: Paula Grasdal

ARCADIA ◎

1. Sketch tree and arch designs and set aside. Using a metal ruler as a guide, tear the printmaking paper to size; the artist made 9" × 9" (23 cm × 23 cm) squares. Cut a piece of Mylar film slightly larger than the squares to use as a printing plate.

2. Tear various colored rice papers into fragments. Mix together PVA and paste glue in equal amounts. Use this mixture to collage the fragments to the paper squares. Let dry.

3. Mix the gouache paints with monotype base in colors of your choice. (Tip: Since this process involves overprinting, test how the colors mix when printed on each other.) Lightly brush a color onto the Mylar printing plate, place the plate (paint side down) onto the paper squares, and burnish the back of the plate with a wooden spoon. Varying the colors for contrast, brush paint onto different textures such as cork or wood veneer. Arrange the painted textures on the Mylar plate, place a paper square on top, and gently burnish the back of the paper. Repeat until you have enough paper (you'll need at least four pieces this project).

4. Cut leaf and vine shapes from cork paper, coat them with paint, then print the shapes on translucent rice and tissue papers using the method described above for printing textures. When the paint is dry, collage the rice and tissue paper prints onto the paper squares.

5. Transfer the arch and tree sketches onto the back of two of the printed papers made in Step 3 and cut out the shapes. With PVA, collage the cutouts onto a paper square in a contrasting color, roll with a brayer, and let dry. Cut another square into a strip that will complete the bottom of the collage, and glue all of the pieces to the masonite backing.

VARIATIONS

Create interesting textures by spraying water onto the painted printing plate or by drawing into the wet paint with a dry brush. Instead of a garden, make a mono-print collage that conjures a different ideal place: a beach, a forest, or even a city.

MATERIALS

- ◎ piece of masonite (in desired size)
- ◎ tree and arch designs
- ◎ rice paper in natural and sage colors
- ◎ absorbent printmaking paper (the artist used Arches 88)
- ◎ transfer paper
- ◎ Mylar polyester film
- ◎ gouache paints
- ◎ monotype base
- ◎ textured objects for printing (the artist used cork paper, wood veneer, and mesh)
- ◎ wooden spoon
- ◎ palette knives
- ◎ freezer paper (for paint palettes)
- ◎ adhesives: PVA glue, paste glue
- ◎ basic collage supplies (see page 8)

ꙮ DREAM HOUSE ꙮ

Using found paper and digitally altered images, Holly Harrison created a folk art collage about the perfect home. A bird, an image for the soul, represents the artist; it perches atop a red house styled as an advent calendar. In the windows are dreams: at bottom left, an art photo of the artist with friends to show a life filled with art and friendship; at bottom right, a comic book drawing to represent romantic love; and at top left, a cornucopia of funky shoes. Other images include music paper manipulated to look like smoke, flowers with Elvis Presley heads, and cats peeking from behind trees and out of windows.

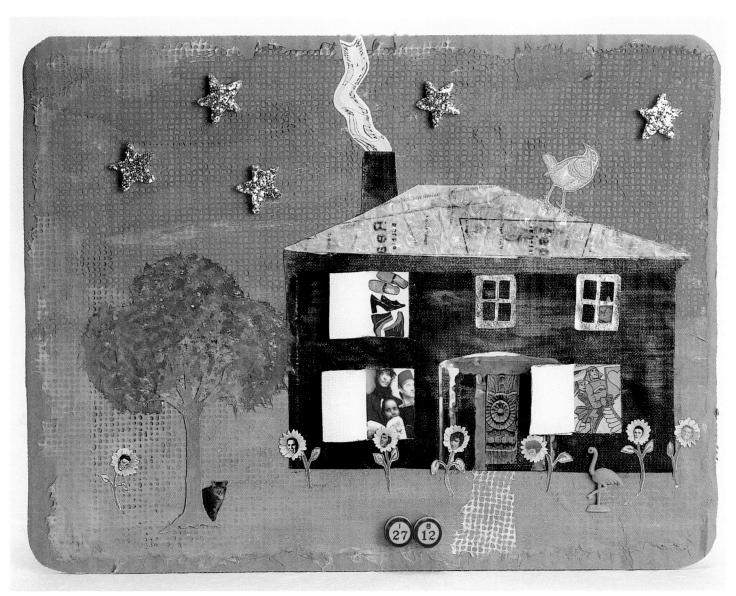

Dimensions: 12" × 16" (30 cm × 41 cm) | Artist: Holly Harrison

DREAM HOUSE ◉

1. Cut a piece of cardboard or mat board to a desired size, and coat it on both sides with acrylic medium. Let dry. Paint a sheet of lace paper with colors for your background (the artist painted a grid-patterned sheet with blue and green acrylics to represent sky and grass). Let dry, then adhere to the cardboard base using acrylic medium.

2. Scan a picture of a house into a computer and in Photoshop, size it and add artistic effects; print out on heavy paper. (Alternately, get the size and effect you want using a color photocopier.) To make window frames, apply gold leaf to craft or art paper, let dry, then cut out frames with a craft knife. Adhere the frames onto the house, then make cuts on three sides for the windows you wish to open.

3. Create images for the open windows by culling through magazines, newspapers, comic books, etc. Cut out images that represent all you could wish for in your perfect home.

4. Create or find images to represent other ideals. This piece uses computer-altered images, a map of New York City on the roof covered by bubble wrap, Bingo pieces for the house number, a plastic flamingo, photographs of the artist's cats, a tree made from painted craft and lace papers, and flowers drawn by the artist and collaged with photos.

5. Once you have assembled your materials, lay them out on the background and move them around until you like the composition. Adhere the papers with acrylic medium and the found objects with craft glue. Hang your collage on the wall and watch your dreams come true.

- ◉ cardboard or mat board base
- ◉ lace papers in varied patterns
- ◉ found papers such as maps, newspapers, comic books, images of a favorite celebrity
- ◉ found objects and embellishments
- ◉ heavy craft or art paper
- ◉ acrylic paints
- ◉ imitation gold leaf
- ◉ glitter
- ◉ digital camera (optional)
- ◉ adhesives: acrylic matte medium, craft glue, leaf sizing
- ◉ basic collage supplies (see page 8)

⊚℘ WORLD TRAVELER'S ℘℘
DREAM MOBILE

Kathy Cano–Murillo recycled free Internet CDs into a whimsical travel mobile. First, she created mini collages on both sides of six discs and dedicated each one to an exotic place in the world that she would like to visit (or revisit): a Polynesian island, Asia, Mexico, Africa, India, New Orleans, and Europe. The travel imagery ranges from realistic details (a tiny shopping bag and actual coins) to fantasies (images of dragons, masks, and beautiful dancers), uniting disparate parts of the world in one imaginative whole, the way multiple narratives are united through the unique logic of dreaming.

Dimensions: 42" × 22" (107 cm × 56 cm) | Artist: Kathy Cano-Murillo

STEPS

1. Cover the CDs on both sides with decorative papers and add collage elements as desired. With hot glue, trim the discs with beads. Drill a hole at the top and bottom of each disc.

2. Drill a hole in the center and at both ends of each dowel. Cut two 30" (76 cm) lengths of twine. Thread each through an end hole in the long dowel, leaving 10" (25 cm) dangling. Knot the twine on both sides of the dowel to hold in place. Bring the longer pieces up, knot them together at 10" (25 cm), and tie them onto a ring for hanging. Thread a dangling end through the center hole of each short dowel, securing with knots, to attach the short dowels beneath the longer one.

3. Cut a 5" (13 cm) length of twine. Thread it through the center hole of the long dowel so it hangs down, and secure with knots. Cut four 8" (20 cm) lengths of twine. Thread them through the four end holes in the short dowels so they hang down; secure with knots.

4. With wire cutters, snip eighteen 4" to 5" (10 cm to 13 cm) strips of copper wire. Bend them into decorative S-shaped swirls with needle-nose pliers. Hook the swirls through each hole in each disc. Attach four discs to the short dowels, using a second copper swirl to connect a disc's top swirl to the twine.

5. For the centerpiece, snip an 8" to 10" (20 cm to 25 cm) strip of wire and make a large decorative swirl. Connect two discs together as shown and attach them to the twine dangling at the center, using the large swirl and another tiny one, if needed. Adjust the twine so the central element hangs slightly below the others. Attach ribbons as shown. Trim the tops of all the dowels with beads.

MATERIALS

- ☺ 6 CDs
- ☺ assorted images, stamps, and tiny trinkets of locations you would like to visit someday
- ☺ decorative papers such as stationery or wrapping paper
- ☺ 6 to 8 strings of Mardi Gras beads
- ☺ colorful glass pebbles
- ☺ sixteen 24" (61 cm) strips of brightly colored ribbon
- ☺ one 1" (3 cm) dowel, 16" (41 cm) long
- ☺ two 1" (3 cm) dowels, 8" (20 cm) long each
- ☺ spool of strong, thin twine
- ☺ spool of copper wire
- ☺ large metal ring (for hanging)
- ☺ handheld drill
- ☺ wire cutters
- ☺ needle-nose pliers
- ☺ adhesives: industrial-strength craft glue, hot-glue gun
- ☺ basic collage supplies (see page 8)

TIP

Stick with light collage objects. When finished, hang the mobile to check it for balance. If there is tilting, glue colored glass pebbles to discs as needed to correct.

USING SYMBOLS IN COLLAGE

B Y ITS VERY NATURE, collage encourages intriguing juxtapositions of images and is for this reason an excellent medium for exploring their symbolic meanings. In "Ceremonial Figure I" (page 51), Lynne Perrella turns a simple archival image of a face into something magical and evocative by collaging it onto a winged torso. The same face in any number of different contexts would have a different effect—surreal if perched on a doll's body, sinister if peering out of a dark archway, mysterious if hidden by veils of translucent tissue paper.

Using layers of images or symbols can help build up a narrative about a particular project's theme. In "The Chess Lesson" (page 36), Paula Grasdal uses a chessboard as the base pattern of a collage about her father, who loved the game. Found objects represent game pieces and act as deeper symbols: A metal crown stands not only for the king, but for kingly attributes such as strength of character that the artist associates with her father.

When looking for symbols to use in artwork, one of the richest sources surrounds us: the world we live in. Often without realizing it, we internalize cultural interpretations of elements both natural and constructed. The red rose is for love, the white for purity; a lighthouse offers safety, a tower entrapment and isolation. By tapping into these archetypes, artists can put together a personal lexicon of symbols to use while working. The effective use of symbols is a powerful tool. Some artists, such as Chantale Légaré (pages 21 and 112), create a unique symbol system that alludes to their vision of the world and forms a cohesive body of work.

The box on the following page lists a variety of symbols (some appear in collages in this book) that might be useful to you. Or if you are in search of more inspiration, try thumbing through books that deal with systems of symbols such as alchemy, Tarot, the Kabbalah, hieroglyphics, dream interpretation, numerology, or heraldry.

A Short Lexicon of Symbols

Architecture

DOORWAY OR GATE—passage, transition

FOUNTAIN—eternal life; in dreams: secrets of the unconscious

HOUSE—psyche, dwelling of soul

ROOF—feminine, sheltering principle

STAIRS—steps in spiritual development, passage of life to death to immortality

WALL—strength, containment

WINDOW—eye of the soul, consciousness, perception

Colors

BLACK—in West: death and mourning; Hindus: time; Egyptians: rebirth and resurrection

BLUE—spirit, intellect; poet Wallace Stevens used it to symbolize imagination

BROWN—earth, autumn

GOLD—perfection, knowledge

GRAY—penitence, humility

GREEN—life, nature; can be jealousy

ORANGE—flames, pride, ambition

PINK—flesh, emotions, heart

PURPLE—royalty, pride, truth

RED—life force, blood; Chinese: good luck; also courage, love

SILVER—linked to moon, magic; Christianity: purity, chastity

VIOLET—most mystical color; also sorrow and mourning

WHITE—purity, perfection, sacredness; Asia: color of mourning

YELLOW—faithlessness, betrayal; when associated with sun: illumination, light, and intellect

Human body

FOOT—balance, freedom of movement

FOOTPRINT—leaving one's mark

HANDS—open, palms up: welcome; folded: submission; raised to head: thought

HEART—love, compassion

Nature

BAT—darkness and chaos in some cultures; Chinese: good luck, longevity

BEES—immortality

BIRD—the soul; can represent angels

BUTTERFLY—metamorphosis, rebirth

CROW—Western: ill omen; Native American: the creative principle; African: guide, messenger of the gods

DRAGONFLY—regeneration, change; Chinese: instability

EGG—origins, beginnings, hope, immortality

ELECTRICITY—creative energy

ENTWINED SNAKES—dual creative forces (good and evil)

FOREST—darkness, chaos, uncertainty; in psychology: the unconscious

GARDEN—paradise

GRIFFIN—vigilance, vengeance, wisdom

LOTUS—ancient Asian symbol for enlightenment

MOON—female sign, resurrection, cyclical nature of things

SCARAB—Egyptian symbol of renewal and regeneration

SUN—male sign, active, creative energy

ORCHID—Chinese symbol of perfection

PEGASUS—speed, desire to fly

PHOENIX—immortality; also gentleness

PINEAPPLE—hospitality

SALMON—Celtic symbol of prophecy and inspiration

TREE OF LIFE—perfect harmony

Objects

ANCHOR—stability, safety

CUP—symbol of feminine realm

HOURGLASS—mortality, passage of time

KEY—power to open things, symbol of wisdom

MIRROR—reflection, self-knowledge

THREAD—life, human destiny

Shapes

CIRCLE—infinity, eternity

CONCENTRIC CIRCLES—the cosmos

SPIRAL—vortex of energy (masculine and feminine); in dreams: growth, need for change

SQUARE—dependability, honesty, safety; Hindu: order, balance of opposites

TRIANGLE—the trinity; pointing up: ascent to heaven (male principle); pointing down: grace descending (female principle)

For more on symbols and their meanings, see *The Encyclopedia of Dreams* by Rosemary Ellen Guiley, *The Illustrated Book of Signs and Symbols* by Miranda Bruce-Mitford, and *The Secret Language of Symbols* by David Fontana.

Chapter Four

☺ INSPIRED BY ☺ NATURE

Because of the prominent use in collage of printed materials and its presence in urban art movements such as Dadaism, Surrealism, and Cubism, we don't always associate this medium with nature or the natural world. Much of what comes to mind when we think "collage" is characterized by the use of symbols, advertising images, typefaces, newspaper clippings, and the like. But there was also an earlier form of collage, when Victorian gentlewomen with time on their hands made elaborate paper constructions layered with flowers, butterfly wings, and feathers. And closer to this century, there's the notable use of sand, leaves, bark, and other natural materials by such painters as Jean Dubuffet and Max Ernst, as well as the iconoclast Joseph Cornell's visual references to astronomy and his longtime fascination with birds.

Just as the advertising images and pop-culture references of the urban aesthetic connect viewer and artist to a whole cultural dimension, natural materials link us to a world of symbols and archetypes that have meaning across many cultures. A branch might represent a tree and symbolize the tree of life. A lotus is not only a beautiful flower, but it is the Eastern symbol of enlightenment. A moonstone is a stone, but as a "tiny moon" it also taps into the many myths and associations that the moon carries across cultures: feminine power, the mystery of creation, cycles of life and death. The artists whose works are in this chapter, whether they use organic materials or simply take their inspiration from nature, all play with the symbolic meanings that are attached to the items or images they use. For example, in "Shhh…" (page 73), Sandra Salamony uses an actual speckled egg along with photocopied images of the egg, and so provides us with both the object and an abstraction of the object. In a sense, she invites us into her process by making an almost casual reference to how art (or artifice) can alter our perceptions of what we see in the world.

The artist who uses nature as his or her starting point, whether as a source of materials or of inspiration, will inevitably end up commenting in some way on the relationship between humanity and nature. Amy Kitchin's "Lilies of the Valley" (page 82), with its fragile bird's nest holding a snake-like fishing lure, hints at an uneasy coexistence of people and the natural world, where a place of refuge gives shelter to a hunter's discarded tool. Offering a radically different take, Karen Michel's "Urban Birdsong"(page 79) shows wise-eyed, singing birds that have adapted to the limitations of their urban environment. Her piece celebrates the power of nature and its ability to regenerate and flourish, even under extreme conditions.

Organically inspired or constructed collages and assemblages reflect another human creation: the garden, a part of nature that has been altered by the human hand and imagination. You might model a piece after a walled medieval garden, an elaborate maze or a simple Zen rock garden. Paula Grasdal created "Secret Garden" (page 70) using images of botanical fragments, lattice screens, a "lost" key, and a patinaed archway, and offers us a fleeting glimpse into an opulent, forgotten courtyard. Though we're always trying to tame nature and impose order on it, once neglected, things revert back to wildness and disorder.

If you watch children outside, you quickly realize that the urge to collect objects is a powerful, inborn one. Shells and sea glass at the beach, small rocks, flowers, and colorful leaves in a garden—these items quickly fill their hands and pockets. And what could be more natural when you find an abandoned bird's nest than to take it home and put it in a shoebox for safekeeping? So we begin to make our first assemblages, which later at school become more formal dioramas, complete with themes and lots of glue.

These early memories of collecting and creating are something we can bring to the making of nature collages and assemblages. Additionally, working with natural materials is satisfying on a visceral level. When we handle feathers, twigs, shells, or sand, we experience ourselves as part of the natural world. And using an actual flower in place of a painted or drawn one creates an immediate link between the art, the viewer, and nature. These are things that are already familiar to us, yet in collage we see them anew through the artist's eyes.

Nature also provides a rich world of color and texture from which an artist can draw inspiration. Try taking the colors from a single rock or a field of flowers as the palette for a collage and you'll discover unimaginable color combinations and hues. Or use the textured surfaces of tree bark and heavily veined leaves to make rubbings for printed-paper collages. There's no end to the variety you'll find in nature, and the challenge is figuring out creative ways to make use of that abundance.

The collage artist who works with (or from) natural materials creates a macrocosm that is a miniature reflection of our world, with one important difference—it can have its own set of rules. In your created world, you can subvert or ignore the laws of nature, letting water exist above sky or letting water and fire occupy the same space. Playing with scale allows large flowers to tower over tiny human figures or stars and dragonflies to coexist. In your world-within-a-box, birds can wear haloes, gardens can keep secrets, and the seasons can be held in permanent suspension. The only limitations, really, are the boundaries of your imagination and the strength of your glue.

When you are foraging for materials outside, whether at the beach or in a forest or meadow, harvest responsibly. Scavenge bark and twigs from the ground rather than living trees, pick flowers only where they grow in abundance (or buy them fresh at a florist or dried at a craft store), and avoid endangered plants. Never take a seemingly unused bird's nest with you in spring—it just might be someone's home.

❧ SECRET GARDEN ❧

For this nature collage, Paula Grasdal combined layers of rice paper, mesh, and cutout paper shapes to create the impression of a light-filled garden glimpsed through a doorway. A single tree graces the site and from its branches hangs a mysterious key, possibly a symbolic reference to the Tree of Knowledge. Insects and plants (tinted photocopies integrated through washes of acrylics) hover nearby. The layers tell a story about making the piece but also convey the idea of a hidden garden, transformed by years of growth and neglect. Perhaps the key will unlock the secrets of its past.

Dimensions: 12" × 9" (30 cm × 23 cm) | Artist: Paula Grasdal

SECRET GARDEN ⊚

1. If there's a tree you climbed as a child or a garden you once loved, you can capture the memory in this collage. Start by drawing tree and vine shapes on the heavyweight paper; cut them out using a craft knife and self-healing mat; set aside. Fold a piece of mesh (the size of your masonite) in half lengthwise and cut an arch or other framing shape. Coat it with instant-rust patina and let dry.

2. Trace the arch onto patterned rice paper and cut out. Collage the paper arch to a piece of backing paper using acrylic medium; roll with a brayer and let dry. Arrange torn pieces of rice paper and tinted photocopies on the backing paper as desired, allowing the arch to frame them. Collage the papers on and let dry. Integrate the paper fragments with washes of diluted acrylics, letting each layer dry before applying more paint. Add a sense of depth by dry-brushing gesso onto raised areas to emphasize the textures. For an aged effect, sand parts of the collage once it is dry.

3. Paint the tree and vine cutouts with layers of metallic gold acrylic and a light topcoat of dry-brushed gesso. Glue them to the collage and roll with a brayer.

4. Brush craft glue on the back of the mesh arch and attach it to the paper one, framing the tree. The subtle patterns of the underlying rice paper will show through the patinaed mesh. Highlight areas of the archway with touches of metallic gold paint.

5. Attach the collage to a masonite backing with PVA, roll with a brayer, then coat the back of the masonite with glue to prevent warping. Let dry.

6. Paint a small rectangle of mesh gold and attach it where desired with craft glue; affix the key on top with the industrial-strength glue. Paint the unfinished frame with diluted gesso; sand when dry for a distressed finish. Mount the collage in the frame.

VARIATION

Coat the tree and the area under the mesh archway with imitation gold leaf to create the effect of a medieval icon.

MATERIALS

⊚ piece of masonite (in desired size)

⊚ unfinished pine frame

⊚ heavyweight paper (for background support and the cut-paper shapes)

⊚ assorted rice papers

⊚ photocopies of insects and plants

⊚ rusted key or other found object

⊚ fiberglass door-screen mesh

⊚ rust patina kit

⊚ acrylic paints in assorted colors including metallic gold

⊚ gesso

⊚ adhesives: acrylic gel medium, PVA glue, craft glue, industrial-strength craft glue

⊚ basic collage supplies (see page 8)

❧ ❧ S H H H ... ❧ ❧

The images of an egg, a butterfly, and a child
encapsulate the themes of incubation and
transformation in this collage. Photoshop let
Sandra Salamony manipulate a butterfly scan
into color separations, which she printed onto
transparency paper and sandwiched between
glass. She also printed scanned photos onto
vellum and photocopied an egg in color. Even
with its reliance on technology, this piece has a
predominantly organic feel, which Salamony
established by collaging tea-stained papers and
pressed flowers onto wood panels and setting
them in an antiqued wooden box. The panels are
moveable, symbolizing the many ways in which
development can occur.

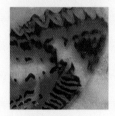

Dimensions: 8" × 10" (20 cm × 25 cm) | Artist: Sandra Salamony

Butterfly photo: Scott Brown

SHHH ... ⑨

STEPS

1. Stain an unfinished shadow box walnut, and antique it using soft white acrylic paint, moss green glaze, and tinted finishing wax (to seal). Once dry, sand along the edges to expose stain.

2. To make the glass tile: Scan a photo of a butterfly. In Photoshop, convert the image to CMYK and separate the channels into four images that will print in each color. Print onto transparency paper. (Alternatively, use a color photocopier to approximate the effect.) Trim to 3" (8 cm) squares, remove the cyan, and sandwich the remaining images between the three glass squares with the black and magenta together and the yellow on its own. Wrap with adhesive copper tape.

3. To make the front panels: Cut two 3¼" × 8" (8½ cm × 20 cm) panels of basswood. Use glue and collage medium to attach decorative papers, pressed flowers, and photocopies to the panels. Stain the papers with tea, and mottle with moss green glaze. To secure the butterfly tile, use brass escutcheon pins (aged in darkening solution). To attach the hollow egg, use a hot-glue gun.

4. To make the see-through panel: Using wire cutters, trim a 4" × 8" (10 cm × 20 cm) piece of hardware cloth. Print a photo on vellum (use a laser printer) and collage it onto the hardware cloth. Let dry. Print a color scan of a flower or other image on transparency paper. Trim to size and staple it to the wire frame.

5. To make the SHHH panel: Cut a 4" × 8" (10 cm × 20 cm) panel of basswood. Print a photo on vellum and collage it onto the panel. Let dry. Stamp letters using the wooden type and sepia calligraphy ink. Wrap hardware cloth or other embellishment around the bottom.

6. Assembling: Paint the ¼" × ¼" (½ cm × ½ cm) basswood strips with soft white acrylic paint and cut into eight 8" (20 cm) lengths. Glue into the box to create runners at top and bottom, incorporating the panels as you go and leaving room for them to slide. The two back panels share the same runners. Add the type if desired (as shown).

MATERIALS

- ⑨ 8" × 10" (20 cm × 25 cm) shadow box
- ⑨ two 4" × 24" (10 cm × 61 cm) basswood panels, ¼" (½ cm) thick
- ⑨ three ¼" × ¼" (½ cm × ½ cm) basswood strips, 24" (61 cm) long
- ⑨ wooden type to spell a word or sound
- ⑨ embellishments such as a speckled egg, pressed flowers, photographs
- ⑨ assorted papers (the artist used wall paper, transparency paper, cream vellum, natural bark paper, and acid-free tissue paper)
- ⑨ hardware cloth
- ⑨ three 3" (8 cm) squares of glass, 1/16" (⅛ cm) thick
- ⑨ self-adhesive copper metal tape
- ⑨ walnut stain
- ⑨ soft white acrylic paint
- ⑨ moss green glaze
- ⑨ tinted finishing wax
- ⑨ sepia calligraphy ink
- ⑨ brewed black tea
- ⑨ four brass escutcheon pins and brass-darkening solution
- ⑨ handheld saw
- ⑨ adhesives: PVA glue, hot-glue gun, collage medium (an equal mix of acrylic matte medium and water)
- ⑨ basic collage supplies (see page 8)

❧ ❧ STRATA ❧ ❧

This collage combines the techniques of frottage (taking a rubbing of a textured surface to create a design) and tissue-paper lamination to create layers of subtle color and texture. To establish the delicate color fields, Paula Grasdal tinted white tissue paper with water-mixable oil paints. She then encapsulated images of ammonites between layers of painted tissue, creating the look of fossilized impressions found in the earth's strata. The difference is that the translucency of the paper allows us to look within the layers to see the treasures buried there.

Dimensions: 6 ½" × 13" (17 cm × 33 cm) | Artist: Paula Grasdal

STRATA ⊚

STEPS

1. Cut out a selection of photocopied images and lightly tint them with diluted water-mixable oil paint. Place the white craft tissue over leaf skeletons (or other natural objects) and rub with the side of a wax crayon to create textures. Make several rubbings.

2. Place the rubbings on freezer paper and tint them with diluted water-mixable oil paints (the artist used yellow ochre, cadmium orange, phthalo green, and olive green). Leave some rubbings untinted for use in Step 5.

3. Cut two pieces of white craft tissue (the size you will want the collage to be) and place one on a piece of freezer paper. Coat it with diluted PVA glue using a wide foam brush, and place the second piece on top, flattening air bubbles with a brayer. Let dry.

4. Rip the tinted tissue into manageable sizes. Working a section at a time, brush glue onto the prepared backing tissue and press the ripped pieces onto the glued area. Let dry.

5. Glue your chosen images in place and paint diluted glue on the central portion of the collage, leaving a 1" (3 cm) border. Place a white piece of tissue onto this central area and roll with a brayer. Layer several untinted rubbings on the surface so that they overlap the images. Coat the collage with diluted glue to make the tissue more translucent.

6. When the tissue has dried, highlight surface textures with oil pastels and define the outside edges with gold oil pastel.

VARIATIONS

Encase metallic thread or natural materials such as feathers between the tissue layers. Create a memory collage by substituting copies of family photographs for the fossils. If you wish, you can use liquid acrylics and matte medium instead of the water-mixable oil paints and PVA glue.

MATERIALS

- ⊚ white craft tissue
- ⊚ photocopies of fossils
- ⊚ leaf skeletons (for rubbings)
- ⊚ water mixable oil paints in various colors
- ⊚ oil pastels
- ⊚ black wax crayon
- ⊚ freezer paper
- ⊚ adhesive: PVA glue
- ⊚ basic collage supplies (see page 8)

⚲⚲ URBAN BIRDSONG ⚲⚲

A mixed-media collage mounted on wood, Karen Michel's colorful piece celebrates the adaptability of nature. Using water-soluble oil pastels, watercolor pencils, and gesso, she created four brightly pigmented landscapes with scratched-away city skylines. These—rather than the blue-sky background—are home to birds sporting oddly human eyes (in fact, cutouts from magazines). By adapting themselves to their city home, these humanized birds, with their shiny paper hearts and painted haloes, are able to survive, even thrive, in the urban world.

Dimensions: 17 ½" × 12" (44 cm × 30 cm) | Artist: Karen Michel

STEPS

1. Cut a piece of wood to size and prime it with a generous layer of gesso. Once the gesso is dry, apply water-soluble oil pastels, working well into the surface with a wet paintbrush. Add more water and pastel as needed to get desired surface.

2. Cut the paper to prepare the individual collages. There are no limits to the possibilities this project offers: The work can be made of many small collages, a few larger ones, or one big one. You can also use as many eyelets as you like.

3. For each collage, prepare the paper surface with a layer of gesso. Once the gesso is dry, begin drawing. Sketch with a pencil first and then work the background with various colors using water-soluble oil pastels. Scratch into the background to achieve desired effects. For the bird's eyes, the artist used human eyes cut out of magazines, which she applied to the surface with acrylic medium.

4. Once the collages are complete, insert eyelets into the corners. Lay the collages out on top of the wood with a dab of acrylic medium on the back to hold them in place. Once you are happy with the layout, gently hammer a short nail into the wood through each eyelet. You can now go back into the wood background and rework the surface or add additional composition elements to the work.

MATERIALS

- ⑤ sheet of wood (in desired size)
- ⑤ paper for individual collages
- ⑤ magazine clippings
- ⑤ water-soluble oil pastels
- ⑤ watercolor pencils
- ⑤ gesso
- ⑤ eyelet pliers and small eyelets
- ⑤ short nail tacks
- ⑤ adhesive: acrylic matte medium
- ⑤ basic collage supplies (see page 8)

TIP

Avoid acrylic gesso: The finish dries glossy and makes it more difficult to work pigments into; sandable hard gesso works best. When working large areas with water-soluble pastels, dip the pastel in water and work it from its side across your surface, dipping as often as needed. Acrylic matte medium will seal and make your collage reworkable without a shiny, high-gloss glare.

❦ LILIES OF THE VALLEY ❦

Made of natural found objects, an old fishing lure, and a graphite drawing by the artist, this piece was inspired by Amy Kitchin's childhood memories of growing up in a house surrounded by woods, hills, creeks, and bridges. Deceptively simple in its wooden box decorated with dried flowers, the assemblage juxtaposes the natural (a cozy bird's nest) with the manufactured (a wooden fishing lure) to create a sense of tension. Though the effect is of a harmonious whole, we quickly realize that the snake-like fishing lure has found its way into a place meant for refuge and safety.

Dimensions: 15" h × 5" w × 3" d (38 cm x 13 cm × 8 cm) | Artist: Amy Kitchin

STEPS

1. The artist began with a small graphite drawing done on vellum. Find or make something similar. If you have an image you like and want to transfer it onto vellum, you can use a photocopier. Tearing the edges of the drawing will create a sense that it is a fragment of a memory. To prevent smudging, spray fixative on the drawing.

2. Paint the inside and outside of the box, and then adhere the vellum drawing inside using acrylic medium as both glue and a sealant. Because vellum is translucent, you can also collage leaves or other flat objects underneath.

3. Arrange and glue the various found objects to the inside and outside of the box. If you use a bird's nest as one of your found objects, glue a small square of paper onto the bottom to help preserve the structure before gluing the whole thing into the box.

4. To adhere objects to the nest (such as the fishing lure), use a thin wire instead of glue, which will mat the nest. Make a tiny hole in the back of the box with a hammer and nail. Wrap the wire around the lure, and then thread both ends of the wire through the back of the nest and through the hole. Secure the lure to the box by twisting together the ends of the wire.

5. Add dried flowers, wood pieces, and other embellishments as desired, inside and out.

MATERIALS

- ☺ old wooden box
- ☺ found natural objects such as willow branches, a bird's nest, bay leaves, dried flowers
- ☺ found wooden objects (the artist used pieces from a drying rack and an old fishing lure)
- ☺ vellum
- ☺ acrylic paints
- ☺ fixative spray
- ☺ wire
- ☺ adhesives: acrylic matte medium, PVA glue (such as Sobo), industrial-strength craft glue
- ☺ basic collage supplies (see page 8)

TIP

Be creative and thoughtful about the way you adhere or attach objects into a space. You can sew objects into place, attach them with hinges, or wrap and tie them with string, wire or fabric. Glue isn't always the best option.

PHOTO TRANSFERS FOR COLLAGE

PAULA GRASDAL

Vintage photographs, memorabilia, and old etchings add character to a collage project, but what if you want to preserve these objects? Photo transfers produce intriguing results and are a way to incorporate one-of-a-kind items in a project without parting with precious originals. Almost any image can be photocopied and transferred onto an absorbent surface such as canvas, silk, paper or spackling using solvent or acrylic medium.

SOLVENT TRANSFERS

Solvent transfers have a dreamlike quality, which lends itself beautifully to memory collages. This technique works best on natural fibers such as paper, silk, or cotton and is effective on absorbent surfaces such as spackling or joint compound. To make a solvent transfer with nontoxic oil of wintergreen (available at pharmacies), place a photocopy of your image face down on paper or fabric and secure it with tape. Dip a cotton swab in the oil and coat the back of the photocopy. Burnish with a bone folder to transfer the image, and lift a corner of the paper to check its progress (repeat if necessary). Experiment with solvent transfers on sheer silk organza, craft tissue paper, and rice paper to use when layering images in your collages. Overlays of translucent images can introduce a mysterious and subtle atmosphere.

ACRYLIC MEDIUM TRANSFERS

Acrylic medium transfers produce a crisp image and can be tinted with diluted acrylic paints. As this process involves water, you'll need to use a fabric or watercolor-paper support. Brush a thin layer of acrylic matte medium onto a fresh black-and-white photocopy, set aside, and brush medium onto the fabric. Place the coated photocopy image side down on the coated fabric, and smooth out air bubbles with a brayer. Let dry for 24 hours, and then soak the joined fabric and paper in tepid water until the paper becomes soft. Gently abrade the paper with a sponge to reveal your image, now in reverse, on the fabric. Tint as desired with paints or inks.

COLOR TRANSFERS

Effective color transfers can be made with a color ink-jet printout and acrylic matte medium. Print out a scanned image or a digital-photo collage. Coat the printout and the support with acrylic medium and follow the directions above. When done on tumbled marble tiles or plaster-coated paper, this technique produces an effect that is reminiscent of fresco painting.

Heat transfer paper is a fast and easy way to adhere color images to fabric or heavy paper. With a color photocopier, copy an image or design on the transfer paper. Trim the paper to size and iron, image side down, onto the support using the manufacturer's instructions for heat settings and time. Peel off the backing paper to reveal the design.

For examples of transfer techniques, see pages 36, 48, and 126. For information about manipulating photocopies for collage, see *The Art and Craft of Collage* by Simon Larbalestier.

Chapter Five

CREATING VISUAL MEMOIRS

WHEN YOU REMEMBER a place or an event, it's not just the visual picture that comes to mind. The scent of freshly cut grass, the feel of the sun on your shoulders, the sound of a lawn sprinkler off in the distance—when these fragments of sensory information come together, they build a more complete and vivid memory of a summer day. In the same way, the collage artist takes fragments in hand— a section of a map, old photographs, scraps of joss paper— and joins them to create an evocative whole. One might say no subject and medium could be more ideally suited.

Because of the distinct differences in purpose and approach in the making of, say, a scrapbook, and the making of a memory collage, we decided to replace the more commonly used description "memory keeping" with "visual memoir." The scrapbook maker seeks to commemorate an event as it occurred, using ephemera such as menus, pressed flowers, ticket stubs, and photographs to faithfully preserve a memory. The collage artist seeks instead to recall the essence of an event, capture its mood or re-create its ambiance. And quite likely the artist will even take liberties, such as replacing people's heads with those of animals or playing with scale and color, abandoning straight storytelling in favor of communicating a personal vision.

Unlike artists working in other media who create representations (whether abstract or realistic) of objects in their work, the collage artist can use the actual object in a piece. This is a great advantage for visual memoir, in that

an object can itself act as a sort of trigger of sensory memory. For example, in "Tuscan Memory Box" (page 88), Paula Grasdal includes an old metal key (located on the inside of the box lid, see photo inset, page 90) in a work that features numerous images of porticos and gates. Not only does this play on the conceit of a key unlocking the door to memory, but the key itself is tangible, rust and all, evoking memories of other keys one might have held or seen. Looking at the collage, you not only take in the portal imagery, but you almost feel the weight of the key in the palm of your hand; by integrating the actual object, Grasdal creates a simple and direct connection between the viewer and her work.

Additionally, old objects are just that—old. In the nicks and blemishes they carry, we see evidence of time that has passed. These objects can connect the artist and viewer with another time and place. Much of the fun in working with found objects is in playing with them, deciphering their stories, imagining them in other contexts, and bringing something of that to your collage. In "Livonia" (page 94), Carol Owen uses many found objects, among them a tarnished silver spoon. By leaving the spoon intact, she both preserves and makes use of its particular past; additionally, she allows the spoon's patina of age to lend the piece a more general historic feel.

What does this all mean for the collage artist? Well, first of all, it means you're not going to want to throw out nifty old clutter that could be put to good use in your art-

capture mood, recall essence
to communicate a personal vision
I can use an actual object to evoke w/sensory memory

work. When the spring-cleaning urge hits, toss any items that seem promising into a shoebox or other container (some artists keep their stashes in meticulously labeled boxes). Hang onto keys, interesting postcards, greeting cards or valentines from friends, photos of events and people important to you, books (damaged ones are great for taking apart), maps, toys (even broken ones), games (the pieces can be used separately), bits of fabric, ticket stubs, programs—really, anything that catches your fancy.

It also means you'll probably find yourself scouring yard sales and junky antiques stores. If something surprises you or makes you smile, grab it. If you find a game you played as a kid, an ad for medicine your grandmother took or a headless doll that's strangely fascinating, buy it. Old photographs are priceless treasures—look for out-of-date fashions, remarkable faces, interesting details that grab your attention. Ann Baldwin uses photographs to great effect in "The Way We Were" (page 91), relying not only on the clothing style and body stance of the people to tell a story, but on the black-and-white imagery, which instantly suggests the past.

Where you can't use old objects themselves, you can still create an aura of age or invoke the past by using techniques such as applying color washes to veil photographs, layering tissue paper to add a sense of mystery, or borrowing the sepia tones from old photos or the washed-out palettes of old Polaroids. Scratching surfaces, adding crackle medium, and crumpling papers are also ways to add the appearance of age.

Finally, try not to over-tell your story—mimic memory's elusiveness by partially hiding images under paint, paper or other images, and emphasizing the jagged edges, the fragmented nature of broken toys or other found objects. Memory is, in essence, romantic—it edits our experience of events as they really occurred, of journeys as they were actually lived—often leaving us with only half-glimpsed fragments, whose power is in their mystery. Collage allows us to compose visual memoirs that reveal specifics of a time gone by or a person loved without abandoning the allure of the mysterious that lets art, and the artist, flourish.

❧ TUSCAN MEMORY BOX ❧

*To conjure up her past travels in Tuscany,
Paula Grasdal mounted four small collages onto
canvas board and housed them inside an
elegantly transformed cigar box featuring a
veneer of Italian maps, patterned vellum, and
paint. An image of a door on the lid entices you
to open the box and enter her Tuscan homage,
which she pieced together using color photocopies
of photographs and found ephemera. Images of
porticos, statuary, and stucco houses were given
an aura of age and mystery by adding layers of
translucent paper and washes of diluted paint.
Scraps of joss paper add a golden glow, perhaps
reflecting the way in which nostalgia often gilds
our memories of a favorite place.*

Dimensions: 9¼" h × 5¾" w × 1¾" d (23½ cm × 14½ cm × 4½ cm) | Artist: Paula Grasdal

STEPS

1. Lightly sand the cigar box and wipe clean. Rip the map into manageable pieces and collage it onto the outside of the box using acrylic gel medium. Burnish wrinkles with the back of a spoon and let dry. Paint with watered-down white gouache.

2. Line the box interior with decorative paper. Cut the patterned vellum to size and collage it to the top of the lid. Paint around the edges with metallic gold paint.

3. Cut out four canvas-board rectangles to fit inside the box and a smaller one for on the lid. Select color photocopies and other collage materials such as stamps, map fragments, and tickets. Arrange the materials on each panel until you like the effect, but do not adhere. Collage on a background layer of decorative paper. Add layers of torn photocopies, ephemera, and torn tracing paper onto the background paper. Let dry. Repeat for the smaller collage, incorporating some of the patterned vellum. Seal the collages with polyurethane.

4. Cover the backs of the four larger collages with decorative paper (the artist used joss paper squares). Paint the edges with metallic paint. Let dry, then seal with polyurethane.

5. Using craft glue, attach the small collage to the box lid. Lightly sand the outside of the box to create an aged effect. Cut a photocopy to fit inside the picture frame and collage it to the inside of the box lid. Affix a rusted key or other found object to the photocopy with epoxy, then assemble the frame and glue it over the photo and key. Place the collages inside the box.

VARIATION

Attach the collages together with ribbon to create an accordion folding "book." Collage color copies onto the outside of a box to create a unique container for found objects collected on your travels.

MATERIALS

- ☺ cigar box
- ☺ canvas board
- ☺ map of a place that's special to you
- ☺ color photocopies of photographs of that place
- ☺ ephemera such as stamps, tickets, brochures
- ☺ decorative papers (the artist used gold joss paper, beige tracing paper, patterned vellum, and cork paper)
- ☺ small gold picture frame with glass
- ☺ rusted metal key or other found object
- ☺ metallic gold acrylic paint
- ☺ white gouache paint
- ☺ matte polyurethane
- ☺ adhesives: acrylic matte medium, acrylic gel medium, epoxy, craft glue
- ☺ basic collage supplies (see page 8)

❧ THE WAY WE WERE ❧

This collage is a combination of scanned photographs and acrylic paints on canvas and was created by Ann Baldwin in memory of her father. Though painted with a loose, easy style, it has a formal feel, established by her choice and placement of photographs. The central image is of her father standing at military attention behind his children. Instead of a joint parental portrait, she used two photos, emphasizing the separateness with a barrier of blue paint. All of the photos are partially veiled with colored glazes, as if we are seeing the family's past through the veil of the artist's perception. Finally, at top left, Baldwin has included an extract from a letter she wrote to her parents as a child. The style is formal and the handwriting neat, indicative of her desire to please them.

Dimensions: 12" × 12" (30 cm × 30 cm) | Artist: Ann Baldwin

STEPS

1. Collect photographs, letters, and meaningful elements to use in your collage. Scan everything into a computer and print out on acid-free paper. Allow the printouts to dry thoroughly for a day. (You can also substitute color photocopies.) Arrange the images and handwritten text on the canvas until you find a placement that pleases you. Adhere with acrylic matte medium and smooth with a brayer.

2. Tear the corrugated cardboard into strips and use them to provide a partial frame for the main photograph.

3. Cover the entire canvas with a layer of matte medium. This will enable you to scratch back into subsequent paint layers without damaging the collaged elements.

4. With a clean brush, "veil" the photos with translucent buff paint. Let dry.

5. Use the acrylic paints to thinly glaze the blank areas of the canvas, cardboard, and parts of the photos, making sure to dry each layer thoroughly before applying the next. The paint should be put on very freely. You might like to add personal thoughts or messages by brushing on an opaque layer of the buff paint and etching in words with the end of the brush while the paint is still wet. Let dry, then apply further transparent glazes of paint. When you have finished, paint the sides of the canvas with black gesso.

6. If desired, brush thick gold paint on the "peaks" of the corrugated cardboard. Finally, apply a layer of gloss medium as a last step to help preserve the photos from the effects of sunlight and to give the painting a light varnish.

MATERIALS

- ◎ 12" × 12" (30 cm × 30 cm) gessoed canvas on heavy stretcher bars, 1¼" (3½ cm) deep
- ◎ reprinted or photocopied photographs
- ◎ handwritten text or letter
- ◎ acid-free paper
- ◎ white corrugated cardboard (craft type or recycled)
- ◎ fluid acrylics in transparent yellow oxide, crimson, gray, and buff
- ◎ tube paint in deep gold
- ◎ black gesso
- ◎ adhesives, acrylic matte meddium, acrylic gel medium
- ◎ basic collage supplies (see page 8)

◎ Ann Baldwin's Creativity Tips

Do more than one collage at the same time. Decide that one is "real" and the other is just messing around. This relieves the pressure of getting it right—and you'll be surprised how often the play collage turns out well. If you become stumped, run an errand, have lunch, and return to your work with fresh eyes. I place my problem paintings in odd corners of the house, where I come across them unexpectedly. In that split second I can view them objectively and often see what needs fixing.

❧ LIVONIA ❧

Embellished with a wide variety of collage
elements such as cancelled stamps, feathers,
shells, a tarnished silver spoon, buttons, maps,
and photocopies of vintage photographs, this
spirit house strongly evokes a sense of history and
place. Always on the lookout for interesting
faces, Carol Owen uses found photographs
prominently in her work. Rather than portraying
specific personal memories, she explores the
themes of family and memories of home in a
more general, universal way. By glazing over the
photos with a color wash, she integrates them
with the background; in this way, they look
almost like the memories of the people portrayed.

Dimensions: 14" h × 12" w × 4" d (36 cm × 30 cm × 10 cm) | Artist: Carol Owen

STEPS	MATERIALS
1. Cut out the foam core to desired shapes (this project is essentially two boxes and a series of lean-tos). Paint both sides of the core with acrylic medium; this will prevent warping. Cover both sides of the core pieces with rice paper, smoothing out carefully to avoid puckering. Let dry.	◎ foam core
	◎ rice paper
	◎ photocopies of photographs
2. Assemble the spirit house using the textile glue. Paint freely with acrylic paints. Let dry.	◎ various print materials such as maps, stamps, music paper
	◎ embellishments such as shells, buttons, beads, coins, keys, jewels
3. Arrange photos and other paper ephemera as desired, then glue down using the textile glue. While arranging the pictures, think about their relationship to each other as well as their placement in the context of the whole. This collage opens to reveal a regal baby at its center, sitting beneath a sun with button rays, on what appears to be a throne of maps, and holding a scepter-like spoon across its knees. The artist has provided a delightful surprise for anyone who looks inside the box.	◎ acrylic paints in various colors
	◎ metallic paints
	◎ adhesives: acrylic matte medium, textile glue, industrial-strength craft glue
	◎ basic collage supplies (see page 8)

4. Glaze over the surface with thin washes of the acrylics and blot. Go over edges of the collage elements and the house with metallic paints or pencils.

5. Embellish with small objects, gluing them in place with craft glue. Use the embellishments to draw attention to certain aspects of the collage. For example, when the door is closed, a handmade wooden frame highlights the peek-a-boo hole in its center. Fences made of pale wood in front of the side boxes serve to enclose the photos as well as to draw our eye to them.

6. Add thick "shingles" of decorative paper to the rooftops. Paint as desired, outlining the edges with metallic paint.

◎ Carol Owen's Creativity Tips

I take workshops and classes and go to seminars in all kinds of different media to keep ideas flowing. One of the most effective tools I've found comes from *The Artist's Way* by Julia Cameron—she calls it "filling the well." I keep binders of clippings of photographs, postcards, articles, and images that speak to me. Flipping through these books always stimulates my creativity.

☙ CLARA ☙

Composed of aged plaster, embossed wallpaper,
found objects, and a vintage photograph, this
multi-media collage has disguised itself as an
antique heirloom discovered in the attic. In it,
Paula Grasdal remembers what it was like to
play at her grandmother's house as a child. The
bottom drawer of her dresser was a treasure trove
of fascinating objects—old buttons, wooden
spools, and beads—a source of inspiration for
childhood artistry. Grasdal chose this photograph
of her grandmother at age five to create a link
between the generations and both of their
childhoods.

Dimensions: 11 3/4" × 14" (29 1/2 cm × 36 cm) | Artist: Paula Grasdal

CLARA ⊚

STEPS	MATERIALS
1. Using diluted craft glue, attach wallpaper and the plaster-coated canvas to a plywood board and roll with a brayer to flatten out air bubbles. Paint the wallpaper with metallic acrylics, wiping away excess paint on the raised areas while still wet. Layer a wash of diluted burnt-umber acrylic paint over the wallpaper and the plaster to create an aged effect. When dry, lightly sand the painted plaster and wipe with diluted yellow-ochre paint.	⊚ piece of plywood (in desired size) ⊚ plaster-coated canvas ⊚ plaster-coated cheesecloth ⊚ strip of embossed wallpaper ⊚ heavy paper ⊚ vintage photograph or color photocopy ⊚ embellishments such as fern fragments, fabric scraps, old buttons ⊚ acrylic paints ⊚ imitation copper leaf ⊚ adhesives: acrylic gel medium, craft glue, leaf sizing, industrial-strength craft glue ⊚ basic collage supplies (see page 8)

2. Mount the photograph or color photocopy onto heavy paper with acrylic medium and roll with a brayer. Create a frame out of plaster-coated cheesecloth and adhere onto the photocopy with craft glue (as a variation, incorporate copies of old letters in the frame). Attach the assembled piece to the painted plaster background with more craft glue.

3. Dab leaf sizing on the frame in a random fashion. Apply the copper leaf with your fingers, using a soft artist's brush to clear away excess (save fragments for other projects). Let dry, and then lightly sand for a distressed finish.

4. Further embellish the collage with found objects that reflect the character of the person in your collage; adhere them with the industrial-strength glue. Apply botanical fragments and fabric scraps with a little acrylic medium.

⊚ Paula Grasdal's Creativity Tips

Surrounding myself with an abundance of found objects and art materials as I work inspires my creative process. Easily reached and visible supplies have a subliminal influence on my artwork; unexpected elements spontaneously find their way into a project, introducing a playful approach. Using what is available in my studio also creates a framework or arena for experimentation, which is invaluable when getting started.

❦ MEMORY OF HOME ❦
FROM AN ISLAND

Candace Walters created this memory painting
with collage elements as an exploration of life's
process. The egg image represents our beginnings,
the portrait of the artist's daughter is the
culmination. In between, there are journeys we
take in sleeping, dreaming, and wakefulness.
Walters playfully collaged images of animals
onto the painting in clusters, almost like thoughts
or memories gathered around her daughter's
head. The animals are speaking to each other
in dialogue bubbles, allowing us to see into the
fantasy life of the daughter as imagined by
the artist.

Dimensions: 32" × 22" (81 cm × 56 cm) | Artist: Candace Walters

STEPS

1. Begin with a strong, heavy paper and set up your work area so your materials are close at hand. Try starting with a wash of a color to eliminate the "shock" and fear of the white paper. Consider a variety of techniques—such as working with a rag or spackling trowel—so that the beginning surface is surprising.

2. Collage found papers onto select areas of the background, then draw and paint images freely, trying not to become specific too quickly. Allow the piece to evolve. Let your ideas and images ebb and flow, disappearing and re-emerging just as memories do. Enjoy the mystery of this process. This piece seems to float between the various images it contains: the painted egg, the collaged talking animals, and the portrait.

3. Working intuitively, build up the piece with more collage materials. Sand back to what's beneath to reveal things; this can be surprising and adds to the visual process of "remembering." The artist refers to this process of adding and taking away elements as the "kitchen sink" method: Throw it all in and then eliminate the clutter to reveal what is rich, provoking, and telling.

MATERIALS

- ☺ pencils
- ☺ pastels
- ☺ watercolors
- ☺ gouache
- ☺ assorted found papers including wallpaper (for the clothing) and pages from old books
- ☺ steel wool
- ☺ adhesive: acrylic matte or gloss medium
- ☺ basic collage supplies (see page 8)

☺ Candace Walters's Creativity Tips

Take a day and visit favorite sources of inspiration—bookstores, flea markets, old photos and scrapbooks, old letters—and enjoy the hunt for materials. A day of this is bound to open up the dreaded block, or what I refer to as "not having an idea in my head." Try out all sorts of experimental techniques as a way of reinventing and re-energizing your creativity. I have even advised my students to run over their work with their car to drastically alter the surface—the result could be dreadful, but it might end up being something remarkable.

TRANSFORMING PAPER FOR COLLAGE

PAULA GRASDAL

DECORATING OR ALTERING PAPER for collage can add atmosphere and character to your projects. Creating your own collage materials opens up a vast array of techniques to experiment with and can be a good way to "get in the mood" to make an artwork. Playing with colors, textures, and materials encourages ideas and inspiration to flow.

PAINT EFFECTS

There are many ways to create painted textures on paper for use in collage. Applying paints or inks with objects other than a brush yields an infinite variety of results. Here are a few ideas to get you started. To create depth: Dip a sea sponge in paint and dab it onto paper in layers, starting with the darkest color and finishing with the lightest. For various mottled effects: Use newsprint to lift wet paint off of painted paper; coat crumpled plastic wrap with a thin layer of paint and stamp onto paper; or paint a variety of colors onto freezer paper, fold it in half to blend the colors, peel apart, and press onto paper.

Monoprinting also produces interesting textures or imagery and can be done without a printmaking press (see pages 54, 57, and 110). Brush or roll water-soluble paints or printing inks onto a printing plate made of Mylar film, place it paint-side down onto absorbent paper, and burnish the back of the plate with a wooden spoon to transfer the design. Other techniques: Before printing, draw into the painted printing plate with a dry brush, press textures into the paint, or wipe off areas with a rag.

MAKING TEXTURES WITH FOUND OBJECTS

Create unique papers for collage using found objects from nature or around the house. For a batik effect: Place paper over a textured object and rub it with a wax crayon or oil pastel, then brush a wash of water-based paint over the rubbing. Stamp designs using found objects such as a string-wrapped block, bubble wrap, doilies, leaves or any other textured item that looks promising. Found objects can also serve as stencils to block out areas of paint and create a negative shape.

ANTIQUING

Many of the collage artists in this book use antiquing techniques to evoke the past. Look at old decaying surfaces for inspiration and try some of the following ideas to achieve a patina of age in your work. Coat heavy paper with plaster, bend it when dry to create cracks, then add a wash of paint. Spread modeling paste or spackling on paper and stamp textures or motifs into the wet surface. Paint gesso onto craft tissue, let dry, then stain with liquid acrylics or inks. Add dry pigments to clear polishing wax and rub it onto painted papers. Tear, sand, or peel papers after they have been glued in place. Brush varnish or crackle glazes over painted paper or images. Crumple paper and spray it with diluted paint to emphasize the wrinkles (brown paper bags work well). This is just a sampling of ways to create striking effects on paper. For more inspiration, see page 133 for suggested reading.

❂ GALLERY OF ❂
INSPIRATION

Dimensions: 32" × 22" (81 cm × 56 cm) | Artist: Candace Walters

MEMORY VESSEL

Candace Walters created this richly textured painting with collage using a process common to much of her work: painting, layering, and unearthing. Working in many layers (using wallpapers, antique handwritten letters, and vintage receipts), she created intuitively, exploring themes related to female mysticism and memory. She then scraped at the surface to reveal images and meanings hidden below. Clear images—the portrait of her daughter gazing at something the viewer cannot see, an egg and its shadow, a shell—are surrounded by a misty veil of color, texture, and partial imagery, creating an impression of memories lingering at the edges of consciousness.

Dimensions: 11" × 8" (28 cm x 20 cm) | Artist: Nina Bagley

BOOK OF TREES

Using diverse found materials, Nina Bagley created a complex accordion-fold artist book inspired by memories of her Southern childhood, when trees were guardians and friends. The base is covered with antique optical testing lenses sandwiched over old photographs of trees. Attached to the base by vintage jewelry parts are six intricately decorated metal panels and a top panel of embossed leather, made from the cover of a Victorian photo album. A treasure trove of findings, Bagley's book is characterized as much by what is hidden as what is visible: a poem tucked into a transparent glassine envelope; a man's face just visible behind metal doors; words etched and pasted onto the backs of things.

BALANCED HEAD

For this hanging assemblage mounted on a wooden cigar box lid, Janet Hofacker was inspired by the combination of the doll's head and wooden exercise tool (they seemed to "just fit together nicely"). By juxtaposing delicate porcelain with a rusted metal plate, she reveals and emphasizes the nature of each. The lightness of the porcelain doll head, tentatively balanced on its wooden wheels, makes a playful statement against the more serious, industrial character of the rusted metal backdrop and heavy spike frame. Glass marbles and pieces of a cut-up collage add visual interest and a further sense of whimsy.

Dimensions: 9" × 10" (23 cm × 25 cm) | Artist: Janet Hofacker

Dimensions: 10" × 6" (25 cm × 15 cm) | Artist: Judi Riesch

ALTERED FACES

Judi Riesch transformed an old wooden address book she found at an antiques shop into this multi-media artwork. She substituted vintage photographs for the existing pages, and reinforced the holes with metal washers. Using acrylic paint, gel medium, pencils, vintage papers, tintypes, wire mesh, buttons, and beeswax, she collaged directly onto the portraits. Riesch prefers to work with actual vintage photographs rather than photocopies because, with their genuine faces captured in time, they provide an intimate connection with the past. Intriguingly, the faces in her book are altered or obscured: Some eyes are blacked out, others peer through wire mesh, and still others look outward with an unfettered gaze.

Dimensions: 6½" × 8" (17 cm × 20 cm) | Artist: Jane Maxwell

MEASURING-UP

⊙

A vintage ledger book, old metal ruler, translucent vellum, and inspiration from doll cutouts are the essential elements in Jane Maxwell's expressive piece about feminine identity. A simple dress form recalls the cutout paper dolls so many women played with as children. Here the meaning is more complex, representing prefab roles shaped by social expectations of how women should act and look. Yet in the details—a lotus blossom struggling to be seen, random drippings of candle wax—Maxwell seems to offer hope that we can shape these forms to suit ourselves.

UNTITLED

The subtle color shifts of this piece belie the many processes and layers Emily Trespas used in its composition: To over-printed layers of transparent monoprints she added chine collé elements and a collaged funnel shape. Inspired by frescoes of the "Life of Saint Francis," in Italy, where she saw what looked like a birdcage with funnel shapes floating around it, the artist created a series of mixed-media mono-prints based on these images. There is a surrealistic discon-nect between the funnel, with its evocation of medicine and measuring, and the birdcage, which speaks of nature and also containment. Here, the funnel shapes exist outside the cage almost like the souls of St. Francis's birds, fluttering between earth and heaven.

Dimensions: 7 ½" × 9" (19 cm × 23 cm) | Artist: Emily Trespas

I'LL GO THERE

Constructed with maps from different countries, the artist's travel photos, and posters of Hindu gods and flowers, Chantale Légaré's mixed-media collage asks us to look at where we are going. She began with a small painting of feet decorated with *mendhi* patterns to symbolize celebrations. Roads sprout out of the feet and lead to two perfect lotus blooms. Map fragments are juxtaposed with the cells of the body to represent sense memories of places and the images, colors, sounds, and scents associated with them. The brilliantly colored landscape is dominated by the lotuses, which symbolize the ultimate path.

Dimensions: 20" × 15" (51 cm × 38 cm) | Artist: Chantale Légaré

Dimensions: 18" × 24" (46 cm × 61 cm) | Artist: Stanford Kay

LOTUS

Working with ink and acrylics on a wallpaper canvas, Stanford Kay created a piece in which a flower sprouts roots reminiscent of the human respiratory system. Using Chinoiserie landscape scenes as a background, he added two collage elements: a color photocopy of a pink lotus blossom, the Asian symbol of enlightenment, and photocopied medieval drawings of buildings placed along the bottom edge. The collaged village puts the floating organ-and-lotus image in context as elevated, much like medieval engravings of botanical studies would float their subjects over a landscape. The artist plays with scale and imagery to create a mysterious world where diverse cultural references converge.

Dimensions: 26" x 28" (66 cm x 71 cm) | Artist: Tracy Spadafora

BULB GARDEN

This piece, encaustic and collage on braced plywood, is based on a sculpture previously made by the artist. She had painted leaf skeletons onto chandelier bulbs and dipped them in beeswax before placing them in a black iron pot filled with pebbles. Working from memory to make this painting, Tracy Spadafora took texts from encyclopedias, novels, and a repeated black-and-white image of a swing and buried them between layers of encaustic paint. The lightbulbs popping out of the pot look like floral bulbs while scales in the background symbolize the fragile equilibrium between humanity and nature.

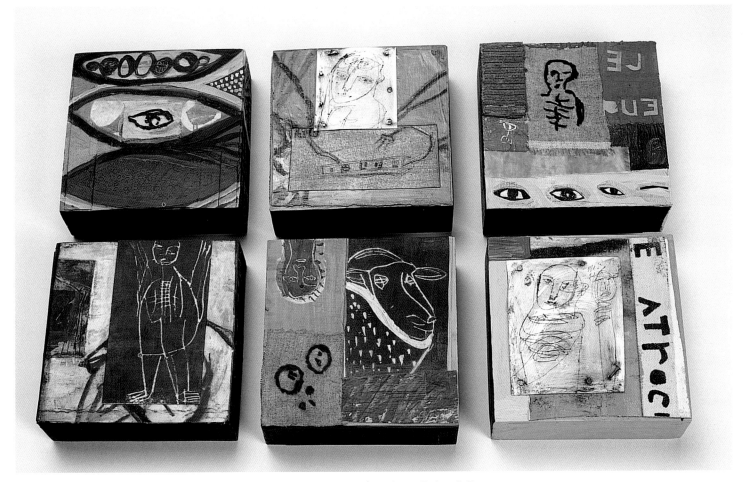

Dimensions: Six 4" h × 4" w × 1" d (10 cm × 10 cm × 3 cm) boxes | Artist: Deborah Putnoi

From left (top row): EYESIGHT, ELECTRICITY, END;
(bottom): RESPIRATION, NEW TIME, ATROCITIES

The collaged boxes in this group are part of a larger series by Deborah Putnoi in which each collage explores a question and juxtaposing them creates a dialog among the disparate elements. For each box, she used a wide variety of materials: pieces of embroidered cloth, canvas with painted text, metal plates scratched with images, scraps of drawings, and colorful paints. The central images—eyes, electric cords and plugs, people's lungs, animals, portraits, pieces of text—resonate in context to raise questions about how we see, the impulses that connect us, our relationship to plants (through breath) and animals, and how we communicate.

Composition XVI   Marianne Fisker Pierce

Dimensions: 24 ½" × 18 ½" (62 cm × 47 cm) | Artist: Marianne Fisker Pierce

COMPOSITION XVI

To explore her ongoing fascination with humanmade forms found in construction machinery and road markings, Marianne Fisker Pierce took a series of photos of the "Big Dig" in Boston, Massachusetts, a particularly complex and dramatic construction project. First, she took endless shots of the machinery and detritus at the site. The rest of the process involved choosing from among the 4" by 6" (10 cm × 15 cm) prints (some of them duplicates), laying them out loosely on a table, and then shuffling and rearranging them until a composition emerged. The result: a quilt-like piece dominated by reds and blacks, held together by the tensions created by intersecting lines and juxtaposed forms.

Dimensions: 19 ½" × 19" (48 cm × 50 cm) | Artist: Tracy Spadafora

UNTITLED

In dream analysis, the image of the house represents the soul or self, as it also does in the work of Tracy Spadafora. She made this monotype with collage using thin layers of etching ink, pieces of maps (in color), and black-and-white aerial photographs of large cities, all of which she applied in layers with an etching press. Through the juxtaposition of these various images, she raises questions about public and private space by positing the role of the individual (house) against the societal demands of an already large world (city) that continues to expand and grow.

Dimensions: 19" × 24" (48 cm × 61 cm) | Artist: Cynthia Winika

SWIMMING I

Cynthia Winika created this evocative collage using encaustic and oil paints, photocopied images from old books, and the technique of scribing a handwritten text into the translucent wax, smearing it with oil color, and then wiping for a drypoint, multilayered effect. The artist likens being under the sea to a dream state, possibly one of mourning. The fish leaping up are emerging from the dream, and the boat represents survival and safety.

THE EARTH ANGEL: PORCH IN SUMMER

Inspired by memories of studying the summer night sky as a child, Amy Kitchin built an assemblage out of a wooden cigar box, foam core, acrylic paints, and natural objects that explores the complex relationships between the smallest natural forms and the vastness of the universe. Juxtaposing seedpods, twigs, and images of dragonflies against painted constellations, she posits the idea that even as we sleep, the universe expands and nature continues to regenerate.

Dimensions: 13" h × 9" w × 2" d (33 cm × 23 cm × 5 cm) | Artist: Amy Kitchin

RELIC IV

In this multi-media fabric collage, Paula Grasdal pays homage to the Cabinets of Curiosity of seventeenth-century Europe: small, personalized museums created by enthusiastic collectors seeking to make sense of the world and its marvels. Typically these cabinets were filled with wondrous artifacts from nature, science, and culture. The colorful piece includes images of fossils, a butterfly, and astronomical instruments, as well as an attached vial of sparkling pyrite. Grasdal used numerous techniques such as photo transfer, appliqué, and machine embroidery to create a richly textured and layered effect.

Dimensions: 17 ½" × 14 ½" (44 cm × 37 cm) | Artist: Paula Grasdal

PRAYER 1

This mixed-media collage, made with gesso, acrylic paint, and watercolor crayons, is part of Karen Michel's continuing Prayer series, which deals with humanity's fundamental dreams and wishes. This particular work has been composed of essential symbols: home, a place of shelter and sanctuary; the hand, or creativity; the moon and ocean for humanity's connection to nature; a lotus, offering hope for enlightenment; the heart, the conduit of love and compassion; and a solitary cell, the artist's reminder that we are one among many.

Dimensions: 26" × 14" (66 cm × 36 cm) | Artist: Karen Michel
From the collection of the Mihale Family

Dimensions: 5 ½" × 7 ¼" (14 cm × 18 ½ cm) | Artist: Emily Trespas

UNTITLED

☉

The pages shown are from an artist's book created by Emily Trespas while she was living and working in Rome. Walking the streets of the city, she gathered bits of paper and labels, peeled flyers from walls, and plucked wrappers from fruit. She frequented the flea market for old photographs to accompany found passport photos. She collaged these artifacts into the book, combining them with colorful painted and drawn passages. A journal such as this can be a wonderful reminder of a trip or serve as inspiration for future art projects.

The pots have
been moved
inside

twilight's
magical light

the gnarled trunk
of an old fig
tree

feet in the
ground
brick path
stones
and leaves

the smell of
cool moist Earth
softly laid to sleep

awaits
another spring

Dimensions: 14" ×11" (36 cm × 28 cm) | Artist: Laurinda T. Bedingfield

SEASON'S END

In this memory collage, made of Polaroid transfers, handmade paper, gold leaf, and acrylic paints on canvas, Laurinda T. Bedingfield looks at death, change, connection, and spring's promise of rebirth through memories of her grandfather. She printed old slides as Polaroid transfers, which gives the images a timeworn, nostalgic quality. The photos record his annual ritual of burying the family's fig trees to protect them from the New England winter and unearthing them again in the spring. One photo shows him digging, another resting. Bedingfield further personalized the piece by incorporating organic material from her backyard, a piece of twine, and a handwritten text.

Dimensions: 9" h × 11" w × 9" d (23 cm × 28 cm × 23 cm) | Artist: Aparna Agrawal

ONE THREAD

Aparna Agrawal created this translucent and delicate sculpture using the simplest of materials: paper, thread, and wax. The organic shape is reminiscent of forms found in nature such as seedpods or egg sacks. Once she had shaped and sewn the paper into a standing tent-like structure, she collaged small rice paper shirts onto the inside surface, connecting them to each other by a single thread. In this way, she relays a vision of the world in which people are individual yet tethered together, belonging to a larger humanity. However, the structure is fragile, the thread is fragile, and so, ultimately, is the connection.

TIME REMEMBERED

༄

Leaving room for people to invent their own narratives is key to the work of Carol Owen and this piece is a prime example. On a base of foam core covered in rice paper, she created a colorful shrine with washes of paint and embellishments such as vintage valentines and postcards, bits of lace and jewelry, and photocopies of old photographs. The heavily collaged and layered piece, with its haunting black-and-white images, offers tantalizing glimpses of past memories and half-told stories, whose completion depends on the imagination of the viewer.

Dimensions: 13" × 10" (33 cm × 25 cm) | Artist: Carol Owen

Dimensions: 24" × 32" (61 cm × 81 cm) | Artist: Rosemary Broton Boyle

UNTITLED

Rosemary Broton Boyle explores the themes of love and romance in this mixed-media collage, composed using layers of various papers, washes of acrylic paints and crackling glazes, and photo transfer techniques. The two deer symbolize a couple settling into the comfort of loving and being loved. Vintage ledger papers collaged on the surface represent love letters and communication while decorative elements such as the leafy embossed wallpaper and translucent rice paper add a romantic Victorian feel.

RENAISSANCE ARMOR

For this assemblage, a papier-mâché dress form collaged with paper and found objects, Janet Hofacker sought to use seemingly useless objects to make a work of art. To create depth, she worked in layers, beginning with torn pieces of parchment paper, followed by tissue paper and sections of lace. Once this first layer was dry, she painted the form using a sea sponge and three shades of diluted acrylic paint. After adding gold-leaf highlights, she let her imagination run wild, gluing on myriad embellishments: tassels, buttons, sequins, junk jewelry, rhinestones, and finials.

Dimensions: 20" × 8" (51 cm × 20 cm) with a 10" (25 cm) base | Artist: Janet Hofacker

BOOKS WILL GET YOU STARTED

☙

Making imaginative use of found objects, foam core, and a photocopy machine, Lynne Perrella reinvented a Victorian birdcage as a playful home for a paper theater. First she repaired the cage and cleaned it up with paint. Then she mounted archival prints of theaters, players, and antique books onto foam core to create the sets and actors, building another platform within the cage so she could house two theaters. The artist has created an atmospheric miniature world that celebrates the history of the English language.

Dimensions: 36" h × 24" w × 10" d (91 cm × 61 cm × 25 cm) | Artist: Lynne Perrella

ON THE BOARDS

Mark Schofield's multi-media assemblage is a whimsical homage to the fantastical eclecticism of the performing arts. Drawing on a wide range of images from dance, performance art, Asian puppetry, poetry slams, and film, the piece is an international stage set with something for everyone to see. Because of its complex layering, Schofield composed the entire piece before gluing. As a final step, he integrated diverse elements—among them moldings, marquee letters, a brass horn, scrap metal, a cardboard jester, a mask, linoleum scraps, various photocopies, an audio-tape reel, and three pennies—using colored pencils, inks, and acrylic paints.

Dimensions: 46" × 34" (117 cm × 86 cm) | Artist: Mark Schofield

BABYBOX DELUXE

Dimensions: 9" (23 cm) tall | Artist: Olivia Thomas

Olivia Thomas transformed a feeling of being overwhelmed into this fun art piece made of a round gift box covered in recycled fabric that she stamped and painted. To this she added a doll's head surrounded by a chaotic heaping of found objects—Monopoly game pieces, dice, seashells, a compass, buttons, holeless beads and pearls, and plastic toys. To represent the many hands reaching out for her, she glued doll's hands to the bottom of the box to act as "feet."

OLD-FASHIONED ROMANCE

Kathy Cano-Murillo created a shrine to all things romantic by mounting vintage Hollywood images and crinkly pieces of tin into a shallow cigar box and garnishing it with loads of rhinestones, paper and fabric roses, glitter, and a lush frame of greenery. Her inspiration: the lustful glances, tender kisses, budding roses, and flaming hearts of vintage Technicolor popcorn flicks.

Dimensions: 15" h × 8" w × 2" d (38 cm × 20 cm × 5 cm) | Artist: Kathy Cano-Murillo

PRODUCT RESOURCE GUIDE

This guide is organized by project and by vendor. Look under the project name to find out about the particular products and materials used, then consult the vendor listing in the right-hand column.

CHAPTER ONE: EXPLORING CREATIVITY

page 18, Temple

Papermaking pulps, felts, and cotton linters are available through Dick Blick Art Materials and at art supply stores.

Sobo Premium Craft & Textile Glue is available at craft stores.

Methyl cellulose is available at Utrecht and other art supply stores.

page 21, Crossings

Lauan (see Glossary, page 9) is available at The Home Depot and lumber stores.

Glass-etching solution is available at craft stores and from Pearl Paint.

CHAPTER TWO: CHRONICLING RELATIONSHIPS

page 30, Pond Life

Encaustic paints and heated palettes are available at R&F Handmade Paints.

page 42, Le Mariage

Handmade paper is available at Twinrocker and art supply stores.

CHAPTER THREE: EXPRESSING DREAMS AND WISHES

page 51, Ceremonial Figure I

Encaustic paints and heated palettes are available at R&F Handmade Paints.

Arches 88 printmaking paper is available at art supply stores.

Lauan is available at The Home Depot and lumber stores.

page 54, Transformation

Rice papers are available at Rugg Road and art supply stores.

page 57, Arcadia

BFK Rives and Arches 88 printmaking paper are available at art supply stores.

Rice papers are available at Rugg Road and art supply stores.

CHAPTER FOUR: INSPIRED BY NATURE

page 70, Secret Garden

BFK Rives heavyweight paper is available at art supply stores.

page 73, Shhh...

Moss green glaze by Plaid and dry metallic pigment in Sunset Gold are manufactured by Pearl Ex. Available at art supply stores.

Brass-darkening solution is available at woodworking supply stores or wherever furniture-restoration supplies are sold.

Hardware cloth is available at hardware stores.

page 79, Urban Birdsong

Portfolio Series water-soluble oil pastels are manufactured by Crayola.

page 82, Lilies of the Valley

Sobo Premium Craft & Textile Glue is available at craft stores.

CHAPTER FIVE: CREATING VISUAL MEMOIRS

page 91, The Way We Were

Acrylic matte medium, heavy gel medium, fluid acrylics (in Transparent Yellow Oxide, Quinacridone Crimson, Paynes Gray, and Titan Buff), and tube paint in Deep Gold are all manufactured by Golden. Available at art supply stores.

Acid-free paper used for printing out scanned images: Strathmore Professional Artist Ink Jet Paper (medium surface). Strathmore Artist Papers are available at art supply stores.

page 100, Memory of Home From an Island

Golden matte and gloss media are available at art supply stores.

The Art Store
401 Park Drive
Boston, MA 02215
phone: (617) 247-3322
art supplies and handmade papers

A.C. Moore craft stores
See www.acmoore.com for store locations.
art and crafts supplies

Dick Blick Art Materials
phone: (800) 723-2787
See www.dickblick.com for store locations or to order online.
art supplies

The Home Depot
See www.homedepot.com for store locations.

Pearl Paint Company
308 Canal Street
New York, NY 10013
phone: (800) 451-PEARL for catalog
art and crafts supplies

Portfolio Series Water-Soluble Oil Pastels
See www.portfolioseries.com or www.crayola.com.

R&F Handmade Paints
506 Broadway
Kingston, NY 12401
phone: (800) 206-8088
See www.rfpaints.com.

Rugg Road Paper Company
105 Charles Street
Boston, MA 02114
phone: (617) 742-0002
handmade specialty papers

Strathmore Artist Papers
See www.strathmoreartist.com for suppliers.

Twinrocker Handmade Paper
100 East Third Street
P.O. Box 413
Brookston, IN 47923
phone: (800) 757-8946
e-mail: twinrocker@twinrocker.com

Utrecht
phone: (800) 223-9132
See www.utrechtart.com for store locations or to order online.
art supplies

INTERNATIONAL RESOURCES

Creative Crafts
11 The Square
Winchester
Hampshire, UK SO23 9ES
phone: 01962 856266
www.creativecrafts.co.uk

HobbyCraft
(stores throughout the UK)
Head Ofice
Bournemouth, England
phone: 1202 596 100

John Lewis
(stores throughout the UK)
Flagship Store
Oxford Street
London W1A 1EX
phone: 207 629 7711
www.johnlewis.co.uk

Eckersley's Arts, Crafts, and Imagination
(store locations in New South Wales, Queensland, South Australia, and Victoria)
phone for catalog: 1-300-657-766
www.eckersleys.com.au

BIBLIOGRAPHY

Bruce-Mitford, Miranda. *The Illustrated Book of Signs and Symbols.* London: Dorling Kindersley, 1996.

Fontana, David. *The Secret Language of Symbols.* San Francisco: Chronicle Books, 1993.

Goldsworthy, Andy. *A Collaboration with Nature.* New York: Henry N. Abrams, 1990.

Guiley, Rosemary Ellen. *The Encyclopedia of Dreams: Symbols and Interpretations.* New York: Crossroads, 1993.

Harlow, William M. *Art Forms from Plant Life.* New York: Dover Publications, 1966, 1976.

Larbalestier, Simon. *The Art and Craft of Collage.* San Francisco: Chronicle Books, 1995.

Leland, Nita and Virginia Lee Williams. *Creative Collage Techniques.* Cincinnati: North Light Books, 1994.

Mattera, Joanne. *The Art of Encaustic Painting: Contemporary Expression in the Ancient Medium of Pigmented Wax.* New York: Watson-Guptill Publications, 2001.

McNiff, Shaun. *Trust the Process: An Artist's Guide to Letting Go.* Boston: Shambhala Publications, 1998.

Rothamel, Susan Pickering. *The Art of Paper Collage.* New York: Sterling Publishing Company, 2001.

Welch, Nancy. *Creative Paper Art: Techniques for Transforming the Surface.* New York: Sterling Publishing Company, 1999.

Wright, Michael. *An Introduction to Mixed Media.* Scarborough, Ontario: Prentice Hall Canada, 1995.

RECOMMENDED READING

Atkinson, Jennifer L. *Collage Art: A Step-by-Step Guide and Showcase.* Gloucester, MA: Rockport Publishers, 1996.

Ayres, Julia. *Monotype: Mediums and Methods for Painterly Printmaking.* New York: Watson-Guptill Publications, 1991.

Cameron, Julia. *The Artist's Way: A Spiritual Path to Higher Creativity.* New York: G. P. Putnam's Sons, 1992.

Eichorn, Rosemary. *The Art of Fabric Collage: An Introduction to Creative Sewing.* Newtown, CT: The Taunton Press, 2000.

Frost, Seena B. *Soul Collage: An Intuitive Collage Process for Individuals and Groups.* Santa Cruz, CA: Hanford Mead Publishers, 2001.

McRee, Livia. *Easy Transfers for Any Surface: Crafting with Images and Photos.* Gloucester, MA: Rockport Publishers, 2002.

Pearce, Amanda. *The Crafter's Complete Guide to Collage.* New York: Watson-Guptill, 1997.

ARTIST DIRECTORY

Aparna Agrawal
16 Crescent Street
Cambridge, MA 02138
aparnaku@attbi.com
www.aparnaart.com

Nina Bagley
796 Savannah Drive
Sylva, NC 28779
papernina@aol.com
www.ninabagleydesign.com

Ann Baldwin
San Rafael, CA
art@annbaldwin.com
www.annbaldwin.com

Laurinda T. Bedingfield
61 Putnam Street
Somerville, MA 02143
(617) 591-8192
pdog@110.net

Rosemary Broton Boyle
Artists West Association
144 Moody Street
Waltham, MA 02459
Phone: (781) 736-0299

Kathy Cano-Murillo
4223 W. Orchid Lane
Phoenix, AZ 85051
kathymurillo@hotmail.com
www.kathycanomurillo.com

Marianne Fisker Pierce
16 Trotting Horse Drive
Lexington, MA 02173
Phone: (781) 862-0640

Paula Grasdal
Boston, MA
paulagrasdal@earthlink.net

Meredith Hamilton
Phone: (718) 403-9755
m.draycott@worldnet.att.net

Holly Harrison
Concord, MA
hoha@mindspring.com

Janet Hofacker

Chantale Légaré
RR 2 Box 999
Vineyard Haven, MA 02568
Phone: (508) 696-3007
chalegare@earthlink.com

Stanford Kay
39 Central Avenue
Nyack, NY 10960
Phone: (845) 358-0798
stanfordkay@earthlink.net

Maria G. Keehan
New York, NY
Phone: (212) 522-1772
maria_keehan@fortunemail.
  com

Amy Kitchin
15 Scottfield Road, #8
Allston, MA 02134
Phone: (617) 566-2183
amy.kitchin@yahoo.com

Jane Maxwell
Newton, MA
janemaxwell@attbi.com

Karen Michel
Phone: (516) 897-3859
kmichelny@hotmail.com
www.karenmichel.com

Carol Owen
Fearrington Post 54
Pittsboro, NC 27312
Phone: (919) 542-0616
gowen1@nc.rr.com

Lynne Perrella
P.O. Box 194
Ancram, NY 12502
www.LKPerrella.com

Deborah Putnoi
Belmont, MA
artforachange@aol.com

Judi Riesch
Philadelphia, PA
jjriesch@aol.com
www.itsmysite.com/
  judiriesch

Sandra Salamony
80 Chestnut Street
Cambridge, MA 02139
sandranoel@aol.com

Mark Schofield
Mark Schofield Illustration
102 First Avenue S., #321-B
Seattle, WA 98134
Phone/Fax: (206) 623-9539
Represented by Sharon
  Dodge
Phone: (800) ARTSTOCK
  or (206) 282-3672
www.illustrationworks.com

Tracy Spadafora
Somerville, MA
spad4@earthlink.net
www.vernonstreet.com

Emily Trespas
180 Main Street
Andover, MA 01810

Olivia Thomas
15441 N. First Street
Phoenix, AZ 85022
Phone: (602) 993-3246
PEZMAN@concentric.net

Candace Walters
c/o Clark Gallery
145 Lincoln Road
Lincoln, MA 01773
(781) 259-8303

Cynthia Winika
87 Hasbrouck Road
New Paltz, NY 12561
Phone: (845) 255-9338
cwinika@earthlink.net
See more of her work (and
  other encaustic work) at
  www.rfpaints.com.

ABOUT THE AUTHORS

HOLLY HARRISON is a freelance writer and editor. Her first craft book, *Angel Crafts: Graceful Gifts and Inspired Designs for 47 Projects*, was published by Rockport in April 2002. She has also contributed to numerous magazines, including *Metropolitan Home*. She and her husband recently moved to Concord, MA, where she finally has a room of her own for writing and crafting.

PAULA GRASDAL is a printmaker and mixed-media artist living in the Boston area. She has contributed to several other Rockport publications, including *Angel Crafts: Graceful Gifts and Inspired Designs for 47 Projects*, *The Crafter's Project Book*, and *Making Shadow Boxes and Shrines*. Her work has been exhibited in galleries in the U.S. and Canada.

ACKNOWLEDGMENTS

WE WOULD LIKE TO THANK EVERYONE at Rockport Publishers who contributed to the successful completion of this project: Silke Braun, Claire MacMaster, Livia McRee, Kristy Mulkern, and Laura Shaw. We're especially grateful to our fabulous editor, Mary Ann Hall, for introducing us and making our collaboration possible, and our publisher, Winnie Prentiss, who graciously stepped up to the plate when Mary Ann was on leave.

We received generous assistance from the following people while we were looking for artists: Kathryn Schultz, the Norma Jean Calderwood executive director at the Cambridge Art Association; Danielle Steinmann, program coordinator in the education department, and Kelly Bennett, program coordinator in the artists department, at the Massachusetts Cultural Council; and Sharilyn Miller, the managing editor of *Somerset Studio* magazine.

Holly would like to extend her personal thanks to her husband, Jim McManus, for his thoughtful feedback and creative ideas; to Kathy Cano-Murillo for her many helpful tips and boundless enthusiasm; to Shawna Mullen for her support and good vibes; and to Paula Grasdal, for her invaluable artistic and editorial contributions and for making collaborating easy and fun.

Paula would like to extend her own thanks to Sandra Salamony for opening the door to the publishing world and for her encouragement; to Selma Bromberg for her inspiring printmaking lessons; and to Holly Harrison for her humor and insight.

Finally, we would both like to thank the artists who contributed their wonderful artwork and creativity. Truly, the book would not have been possible without them.